"Christians need a fresh vision ᴏᴜ ... expands beyond the tired categories of evangelism, ethics, ... *for Better* points that way forward with a thoughtful combination of theology, ..., and narrative. Elaine Howard Ecklund and Denise Daniels' attentiveness to the institutional nature of work makes an especially important contribution. Pastors seeking to help people in their nine-to-five lives would especially benefit from reading this excellent book."

Curtis Chang, host of the *Good Faith* podcast and author of *The Anxiety Opportunity* and *The After Party*

"Elaine Howard Ecklund and Denise Daniels are amazing women who have been working for better throughout their academic careers. In this beautiful, well-researched book, they share significant and profound insights on how to help people of faith feel like they can be whole people at work. The authors move beyond faith *and* work to probe more deeply into more effective ways to embody faith *at* work for the sake of the common good. The book is filled with practical wisdom and will help you as a reader become wiser as well!"

L. Gregory Jones, president of Belmont University

"Elaine Howard Ecklund and Denise Daniels offer a timely and important intervention in the conversation about faith and work, showing how Christians can engage in the workplaces of our pluralistic society not only with faithfulness and authenticity but also with charity and hospitality."

John Inazu, law professor and author of *Confident Pluralism* and *Learning to Disagree*

"*Working for Better* is a groundbreaking book. Elaine Howard Ecklund and Denise Daniels have conducted a seminal study on faith and work—and now they're leveraging their research findings to help the rest of us untangle how people of faith navigate toward better in the face of workplace issues that often feel complex and divisive in today's world."

Michaela O'Donnell, author of *Make Work Matter* and *Life in Flux* and the Mary and Dale Andringa Executive Director Chair at the Max De Pree Center for Leadership at Fuller Theological Seminary

"Whether you are just beginning a career or are a seasoned leader in your field, you will find *Working for Better* is a refreshingly honest and discerning must-read on what Christian faithfulness looks like in today's workplace. Combining data-driven observations and personal testimonies that perceptively bring to light the challenges that many face navigating their work lives, Elaine Howard Ecklund and Denise Daniels are perfect guides for those who long to follow Jesus' way by offering an inspiring call and practical steps to living faithfully through an ethic of radical embrace."

Felicia Wu Song, sociologist and author of *Restless Devices*

"*Working for Better* is a powerful reminder that all work matters to God. With deep insight and practical wisdom, it challenges us to see our daily jobs as opportunities to serve others and reflect God's character. This book will inspire you to pursue excellence and find eternal purpose in your work. I highly recommend!"

Jordan Raynor, author of *The Sacredness of Secular Work* and *Redeeming Your Time*

WORKING
FOR
BETTER

A NEW APPROACH TO
FAITH AT WORK

ELAINE HOWARD ECKLUND
& DENISE DANIELS

Academic

An imprint of InterVarsity Press
Downers Grove, Illinois

InterVarsity Press
P.O. Box 1400 | Downers Grove, IL 60515-1426
ivpress.com | email@ivpress.com

InterVarsity Press® is the publishing division of InterVarsity Christian Fellowship/USA®. For more information, visit intervarsity.org.

All Scripture quotations, unless otherwise indicated, are taken from The Holy Bible, New International Version®, NIV®. Copyright © 1973, 1978, 1984, 2011 by Biblica, Inc.™ Used by permission of Zondervan. All rights reserved worldwide. www.zondervan.com. The "NIV" and "New International Version" are trademarks registered in the United States Patent and Trademark Office by Biblica, Inc.™

While any stories in this book are true, some names and identifying information may have been changed to protect the privacy of individuals.

The publisher cannot verify the accuracy or functionality of website URLs used in this book beyond the date of publication.

Cover design: Faceout Studio
Interior design: Daniel van Loon

ISBN 978-1-5140-1126-3 (print) | ISBN 978-1-5140-1127-0 (digital)

Printed in the United States of America ∞

Library of Congress Cataloging-in-Publication Data
Names: Ecklund, Elaine Howard, author. | Daniels, Denise (Professor of
 entrepreneurship), author.
Title: Working for better : a new approach to faith at work / Elaine Howard
 Ecklund and Denise Daniels.
Description: Downers Grove, IL : IVP Academic, [2025] | Includes
 bibliographical references and index.
Identifiers: LCCN 2025003490 (print) | LCCN 2025003491 (ebook) | ISBN
 9781514011263 (paperback) | ISBN 9781514011270 (ebook)
Subjects: LCSH: Religion in the workplace–United States. |
 Employees–Religious life–United States. | Religious
 discrimination–United States.
Classification: LCC BL65.W67 E237 2025 (print) | LCC BL65.W67 (ebook) |
 DDC 650.1088/27–dc23/eng/20250222
LC record available at https://lccn.loc.gov/2025003490
LC ebook record available at https://lccn.loc.gov/2025003491

31   30   29   28   27   26   25 | 13   12   11   10   9   8   7   6   5   4   3   2   1

ELAINE

This book is dedicated to my mother-in-law Marian Gladys Ecklund (1939–2024), who lived her faith through her work and encouraged others to do the same.

DENISE

This book is dedicated to my adult children, Josh, Samara, Danica, and Zach. May you live out God's purposes through your work.

CONTENTS

Preface

WHY THIS BOOK?

ELAINE'S STORY

I have been journaling nearly every day for thirty years. What would an outsider see in this chronicle of a life? They would know that my work is one of the things at the center of my life. My journal entries have reflected a long-standing desire and sense of calling to work in academia: "Since I sat in the corner of my kindergarten class reading *Dick and Jane* I have loved words and I have loved reading; the place where I have always felt most at home was in the university library, among ideas," I wrote in one green spiral notebook nearly twenty-five years ago, when I was deciding what career steps I would take and was anxious about my future job prospects. "And the people that I have most wanted to share those ideas with is students."

And an outsider would see that I have often struggled to integrate my faith and my work. In one entry, after I started graduate school, I wrote about my experience at an academic conference in a Midwestern venue. It was early fall, with a distinct chill in the air; academics from different disciplines had gathered to talk about faith in the context of work. I was assigned a mentor from a prestigious university who worked in a different field of study. After explaining my idea for a new research project examining how scientists approach religion in their scientific work, research that I thought would allow me to connect my academic work with churches, I remember an odd look coming across his face. It immediately told me I had said something wrong. A bit of a grimace turned to a softer expression as he told me, "I wouldn't suggest that line of study; it will be hard to get a job if you talk so openly about your faith. Wait until after you have job security to talk about your faith. Christians are often discriminated against in universities."

I was concerned about how I could integrate my faith and work life as a university professor and how much I could or should discuss my faith in the course of my research and teaching. Feedback like that from a mentor made me question whether I should pursue research on religion at all during my sociology PhD. To my knowledge, I have rarely been discriminated against in an academic context because of my faith, but it also feels taboo to talk openly about personal faith in most university environments.

Fast-forward. I am now a professor and work with students from many different faith backgrounds and none. My own experience alongside my leadership and mentoring work with students has led me to examine the tensions that arise when the most important and foundational aspects of a person's life clash. What are the consequences when one expresses one's Christian faith (or one's Jewish or Muslim faith, for that matter) at work? Faith can seem at odds with the norms of a workplace. I have learned that, although I still have tensions, I am not alone in struggling with how to thoughtfully integrate my Christian faith and work.

DENISE'S STORY

I became an academic because I was good at school, so I just kept going. Because I was interested in what motivated people at work, I pursued a graduate degree in organizational behavior. I earned a PhD, was hired by a university, got married, and had two babies before I turned thirty. Soon, I found myself both exhausted and anxious about whether the life I was living was really what God wanted for me. While my grad school training had been excellent preparation for a life of research and teaching, it had not prepared me to think through issues of existential purpose, and certainly not issues of religious faith commitments. And while I had been a follower of Jesus ever since I can remember, I found myself feeling unsure about how my Christian commitments should affect my own work beyond being nice to people.

As I struggled with the sleep deprivation that comes with being the parent of a newborn and a one-year-old alongside the demands of a full-time academic job, I found myself unsurprisingly drawn to the concept of sabbath. Because I had been trained as a scholar, my natural inclination was to do some research on the topic. Over the next few years, I published several journal articles on the intersection of sabbath and organizational practice. But more importantly, I began to practice sabbath on a regular basis. This was particularly helpful because my husband and I added two more children to our family during those years.

My own exhaustion and subsequent foray into the study and practice of sabbath soon became an entrée into the more expansive world of faith and work. I saw the ways that my faith commitments were influencing my own work practices, and that made me curious to know more about the intersection between faith and work for others as well.

It also seemed that God was up to something much bigger than me in those early years of my career. The first two decades of the 2000s saw an explosion of faith-and-work ministries, books, and conferences. At the turn of the millennium, there were very few organizational scholars researching in this area. But it was personally and professionally engaging to me.

WORKING TOGETHER

When the two of us met over a decade ago, we were immediately drawn to each other. We had similar backgrounds as Christian scholars in the social sciences, we both had young children at home, and we were both interested in the academic study of how faith makes a difference in people's lives. And both of us wanted to learn even more about how to integrate our faith and our work in these times. We decided to work together on a large-scale project examining how people think about and enact their faith in the context of the workplace but also about how churches and other communities of faith shape the ways people understand their work.

Working together has led us to a new approach that is somewhat different from the many faith-and-work resources available to individuals and churches. Ours moves from an individualized and in-the-trenches approach to an other-focused perspective of radical embrace. We argue that the exclusive claims of Christianity demand an embrace of others, regardless of their faith commitments, belief systems, or worldviews. Our perspective is based on twenty years of research on faith at work and conducting the largest set of studies to date of this topic. But it is also based on the stories of Christians in the workplace we spoke with, as well as our own stories. What is needed in these times is for Christians to develop a deeper understanding of the *imago Dei*—that every person we encounter is worthy of dignity and respect because everyone is made in the image of God. We argue that one of the best ways we can live out our calling as Christians in the workplace is to radically embrace those who are different from ourselves. We integrate the radical-embrace perspective throughout the book, showing how this belief demands different practices and ways of living out our faith in the workplace, practices that move beyond an emphasis on talking about our beliefs or defending our rights. In this current cultural moment, our faith demands fully being present in who we are distinctively while also making the space for others to be fully present in all the fullness of their own humanity.

Just as we have brought our own faith commitments as Christians to how we approach our work, many employees want to do the same. Yet, figuring out how to integrate faith and work is complicated. Both of us would have liked clearer direction on how to best foster faith at work—a data-driven approach. That is what you will find in this book: a research-based examination of how religion and spirituality enter the workplace, how American workers see the connections between faith and work, and how organizational leaders can understand and lead religiously diverse, faith-friendly workplaces.

A FEW ORIENTING COMMENTS

We have written this book together, and most of the time you will hear us talk about our research and findings in the first-person plural (*we/ our/us*). However, there are times that one of us has a relevant personal story to share that is unique to that person. When this happens, we identify which of us had the experience (Elaine or Denise) and we shift to using the third-person singular (*she/her*), to denote that the story is not common to both of us.

You will also note that at the end of each chapter we have provided some reflection questions. Our hope is that these questions will be useful to individuals or groups. Most of these questions are broadly directed to anyone who works. We have listed these as questions for everyone, although some of them may be more relevant for entry-level workers and others more appropriate for those in positions of organizational leadership. In most chapters we also include questions that are designated for faith communities. These questions can also be answered by everyone, but they might be particularly relevant for church and parachurch leaders who are trying to engage their congregations or constituents in integrating Christian faith and work.

ACKNOWLEDGMENTS

MANY HAVE SUPPORTED the research and writing for *Working for Better*. Special thanks to Deidra Coleman, Laura Achenbaum, Hayley Hemstreet, Rachel Schneider, and Heather Wax. Thank you to the (then) students and postdoctoral fellows (many of whom are now professors and professionals of other sorts) who helped with research and analysis: Moses Biney, Dan Bolger, Di Di, Jauhara Ferguson, Jacqui Frost, Kerby Goff, Bradley Johnson, Laura Johnson, Brenton Kalinowski, Bianca Mabute-Louie, Kennedi Macklin, Eduard van der Merwe, Oneya Fennell Okuwobi, Esmeralda Sanchez Salazar, and Simranjit Steel. We also acknowledge Adrian Almy, Aishi Ayyanathan, Adrienne Bradley, Rose Kantorczyk, Shannon Klein, Michael McDowell, Alex Nuyda, Shifa Rahman, Connor Rothschild, Lindsey Schirn, Aditi Velgekar, and William Wang.

We are grateful to our advisory board members for their feedback in early stages of this project: Melissa Alfaro, Katherine Leary Alsdorf, Katelyn Beaty, Luke Bobo, Jim Hackett, David Miller, Richard Mouw, Jerry Park, Alice Rhee, and Mark Roberts. Thank you also to our network advisers: Fernando Cascante, Kevin Dougherty, Kevin Dudley, Michael Emerson, Al Erisman, John Fontana, Brian Gagnon, Kaitlin Hasseler, Greg Jones, Chris Lowney, Gerardo Marti, Mia Mends, Will Messenger, Mitch Neubert, Cathy Nunnally, Steven Purcell, Shirley Roels, Amy Sherman, Laura Sorrell, Michael Stallard, Fernando Tamara, and John Witvliet.

Special thanks to our editor, Jon Boyd, especially for his careful editing hand, and to everyone at InterVarsity Press, but especially Tara

Burns, Krista Clayton, Karin DeHaven, Alexandra Horn, Ellen Hsu, and Shane White. We are most grateful for the support of our families.

This publication was made possible through the support of two grants from Lilly Endowment Inc. ("Faith at Work: An Empirical Study," #2017 0021, Elaine Howard Ecklund PI, Denise Daniels Co-PI; and "The Impact of COVID-19 and Racism on Faith at Work," #2020-1655, Elaine Howard Ecklund PI, Denise Daniels Co-PI). The opinions expressed in this publication are those of the authors and do not necessarily reflect the views of Lilly Endowment Inc.

1

A LOOK AT HOW THE
WORLD IS CHANGING

Joann was worried that if people knew about her beliefs, the door would be closed to any future promotions.[1] When Denise interviewed her as part of an organizational assessment, Joann was a successful midlevel manager. She explained: "I would love to be myself at work. I'd love to be open with people and divulge my whole identity. But I have to be careful to watch what I say; I feel like I'm lying to everyone. I'm generally a very open and honest person, but I have to keep myself hidden here. I don't feel like there's an alternative."

On the one hand, these reflections feel familiar. Many Christians have some concern that expressing their faith at work could limit their opportunities in the workplace. *But Joann was not a Christian.* She was an atheist who did not believe in God or a spiritual realm. Joann was concerned that it was these beliefs that would limit her ability to succeed beyond her current role if she were found out. The founders and current leadership of the company where she worked were all outspoken Christians. These leaders wanted to honor God in their company. They wanted to care for their employees and wanted for everyone in the company to be able to bring their whole

---

[1]Throughout this book we use pseudonyms to protect the anonymity of those we interviewed.

selves—including their faith—to work. But they were unaware of the ways in which their approach to faith in the workplace might be stifling for those with religious identities that were very different from their own.

We have seen how Christian faith lived openly in a workplace can make employees feel cared for and more committed, reform the workplace in helpful ways, foster other kinds of diversity, and facilitate working with others for the common good of an organization. But we have also seen organizations and organizational leaders approach faith through a narrow lens, which leads to substantial blind spots, undermining rather than helping them accomplish their goals.

A NEW APPROACH TO FAITH AT WORK

One of the historical trends that has been both a positive influence and a pressure factor at the intersection of religion and work is the explosion in recent decades of the faith-at-work movement. In the post–World War II boom, evangelical Christians, in particular, began pushing back against the view that ministry was restricted to a full-time calling to a church or Christian organization, and everybody else by default went into the secular workplace, rejoining their Christian fellowship at church on Sunday in order to recharge for their long stretches out in the world. In contrast, the new emphasis encouraged Christians to see their work *as* their ministry, *as* their calling.

Viewing themselves as mostly loners among nonbelievers, these Monday morning believers were encouraged to develop their own personal witness to the world in considering such questions as, What is my role as a Christian in a secular job? How and when should I share my faith? How do I witness without words? How should I treat and be treated by those who don't share my faith? How can I help lead others to faith in Christ? This individualized approach helped reinforce a minority identity, giving rise to concerns about infringements on religious freedoms and experiences of persecution for holding religious beliefs or abstaining from workplace behavior that violated those beliefs.

Although this Christian perspective has tended to distinguish the commercial workplace as a secular setting, this is not really the case. There is a new focus in modern workplaces on bringing our whole selves to work; people of faith increasingly want to express their convictions while on the job. At all levels of business in the United States, employees no longer want to leave their faith behind when they go to work. Nearly three-quarters of Americans are affiliated with a religious tradition, and many feel their religious faith is an essential part of who they are—associated with the deepest values they hold, relationships they forge, actions they take, and decisions they make.[2] And many of those who are not part of religious organizations consider spirituality a meaningful part of their lives and relevant to their work.[3] They want to express this part of themselves in their work life, which dominates the majority of their time.

As workers increasingly bring their faith to work, it creates new challenges for leaders in handling religion in the workplace. Leaders are rightly concerned that employees talking about their faith at work might feel invasive or marginalizing to those who do not share the faith, giving rise to conflict. And while religious accommodations for legitimate expressions of faith are legally mandated, it is often unclear to organizational leaders, amid the many pressing needs of their workplaces, how best to accommodate such expressions.

Organizational leaders need tools for how to foster respectful expression rather than suppress religious identity. The well-being of all workers and the health of organizations is served by religious pluralism, not religious privatization. If organizational leaders want to increase diversity of all types in their workplaces, especially racial and gender

---

[2]Daniel Cox and Robert P. Jones, "America's Changing Religious Identity," PRRI, September 6, 2017, www.prri.org/research/american-religious-landscape-christian-religiously-unaffiliated/.
[3]Jaime Kucinskas, *The Mindful Elite: Mobilizing from the Inside Out* (New York: Oxford University Press, 2019).

diversity, they must also understand how religious diversity is deeply linked to these categories.

The growing pluralism of US society also creates new challenges for Christians at work. Although Christianity is still the largest religious tradition in the United States, workplaces are becoming more religiously diverse, with a growing nonreligious population. In this current cultural climate, our faith demands that we fully live out our Christian commitments while also making space for others to express their own religious or nonreligious identities.

Christians have traditionally expressed their faith at work with a focus on the self: talking about their faith, sharing their beliefs, defending their moral stances, and focusing on their religious freedoms. But there is much less tolerance than there used to be for overt expressions of our faith. How to respect this space while expressing Christian faith appropriately is an increasingly tricky proposition. Christians need a new approach to faith at work that does not compromise their faith while still meeting the moment.

COMPLEXITIES RAISE NEW QUESTIONS

Because the rapid pace of change in US society has exacerbated the tensions already inherent in this arena, we conducted a first-of-its-kind set of research projects to form a data-driven approach to identifying and proposing solutions for the challenge of fostering faith at work. For those who are data junkies, we include several more pages of information about the specifics of our study at the end of the book. Our insights and suggested practices are based on a collective twenty years of research on the faith-at-work movement and how Christians specifically seek to integrate faith and work.

Over the past few years, we have conducted the most comprehensive set of studies to date of faith at work, including (1) focus groups with pastors and congregants in several cities in the United States; (2) surveys of over fifteen thousand workers—before, during, and after the pandemic—who are representative of the demographics of the US population, including those from a variety of faith traditions as well as nonreligious workers; and (3) in-depth follow-up interviews with 287 people, many of whom are committed Christians who care about faith at work. Since this is a book written primarily for Christians, the majority of the narratives presented in this book are from Christians we interviewed, unless we specify otherwise.

Although we come to this topic as scholars, we are also living faith-and-work integration ourselves. In addition to the data, we also provide personal stories from our own experiences since these topics are important for each of us as Christians. The recommendations we make in this book for the tensions we have identified reflect our hope that people of faith will do all they can to help make the world better for everyone, not just for Christians.

Our research has revealed how new demographic realities in American culture are requiring changes in the traditional models of the faith-at-work movement. For example, we put personal expressions of faith such as evangelizing alongside different pieces of the Christian tradition—those that emphasize the *imago Dei*, the idea that all people are created in the image of God. In our interviews with Christian workers, some talked about the importance of this concept for finding meaning and purpose. "If I am created by God, in God's image, in His likeness, and I'm given a purpose, I have a reason for living. . . . I help other people not to make myself look better, or to feel better," a man who works as a village planner told Elaine. A geneticist said he helped others "because [I want to] glorify the one who created me, in his image." In this scientist's view, "we all have that shared calling of being made in the image of God. That's our calling. It's to reflect him. It's to represent him."[4]

---

[4]These quotes are from respondents who were interviewed for Elaine Howard Ecklund, *Why Science and Faith Need Each Other: Eight Shared Values That Move Us Beyond Fear* (Grand Rapids, MI: Brazos, 2020).

These responses reflect a new model of faith at work garnered from a bedrock of Christian theology: *all people* are made in the image of God. The new possibilities arising from this emphasis suggest that in these divisive times of increasingly violent conflict on the global stage, US Christians at work should do more to focus on how others—all of us—are made in the image of God. Expressing Christian faith at work includes constantly looking for ways to recognize the dignity and worth of all people in the workplace and embracing what some think of as "the other"—those who are outside our own faith community. Rather than concentrating solely on the kind of employee we are, our own expressions of faith at work, and our personal responsibility and morality, we can examine the values of the workplace as a whole and work to advance justice, fairness, human flourishing, and the common good.

FIVE KEY TENSIONS

The data we have spent years collecting explores not just Christian faith but also how workers from a variety of religious traditions are bringing their faith into the workplace, the impact this has, and why it is so important to manage and support religious diversity—and its diverse expressions—in the workplace. We explain how those from different racial groups, genders, ages, social classes, and occupations negotiate their faith in the workplace. We especially draw on the voices of women and people of color, who have often been left out of literature concerning faith at work, workplace success, and workplace spirituality.

When we put our research alongside the traditional understandings and approaches that have characterized the Christian faith-at-work movement, five key tensions emerged that show where the gaps are between assumptions and realities. We explore each of these tensions across a pair of chapters describing the pressures building and suggesting how they might be resolved. In every chapter we provide an understanding of current realities grounded in social-scientific data.

Each of our chapter pairings focuses on an older approach to faith at work and then shifts to a newer way of considering our engagement while retaining aspects of the traditional. We work hard as we explain these chapter pairings to amplify what we can learn from the traditional approach while setting forth a new way. We chose these particular chapter pairings in this particular order because this is where— as scholars and as Christian workers ourselves—we think there needs to be the most intervention in setting forth a new vision in order to see the greatest redemption in workplaces today.

In chapters two and three we show that while Christians' understanding of work and calling has changed over time to become more expansive, the message that all work can be done in service to God has not made the inroads we might have expected. We also provide a framework that broadens typical conceptualizations of calling. Chapters four and five examine experiences of religious discrimination and accommodation at work and explore the ways that Christians can move beyond primarily seeing themselves as a persecuted minority to helping prevent discrimination and becoming advocates and protectors of fair treatment for all and, in particular, for those who are outsiders. In chapters six and seven we discuss the ways we can move from focusing only on personal responsibility to leading the way in creating organizational systems that affect behaviors at work for the common good, and we suggest ways people can contribute to structures that are more likely to engender positive organizational outcomes. Chapters eight and nine discuss the different levels of support that working men and women receive from their church communities and how that can affect their workplace outcomes. We provide suggestions for ways both churches and workplace leaders can contribute to flourishing for all. In chapters ten and eleven, our last chapter pairing, we examine the many ways Christians express their faith in the workplace and how such expressions are viewed by those outside the faith. We argue for a principled pluralism approach, which respects those of different beliefs and practices while holding firm to the foundational aspects of the Christian faith.

We end the book, in chapter twelve, with a discussion of how a biblical understanding of rest might infuse the way we approach our work. We intentionally do not include a chapter pairing in response to our chapter on rest. In some sense, the first eleven chapters of this book provide the substance of the pairing for the last chapter. Most of this book focuses on how our faith influences our work. But Christians should also be attentive to how our faith shapes our approach to rest. No matter our approach to faith at work, rest should thread through all we do. To rest from our work and *to cultivate rest possibilities for others at work* reveals our place in the created order. The success of the world ultimately does not depend on us.

FROM DEFENDING RIGHTS TO RADICAL EMBRACE

Our recommended path for resolving these key tensions reflects a fresh model for faith at work that moves from an individualized, in-the-trenches approach to an other-focused, more community-oriented perspective of radical embrace.[5]

More specifically, we make the case that the exclusive claims of Christianity actually *demand* an embrace of others in the workplace, regardless of their faith commitments, belief systems, or worldviews. We call on Christians to bring their faith into the workplace by shifting from an emphasis on talking about our beliefs and defending our own rights to empathizing with those who are religiously different, with a particular emphasis on the *imago Dei*—the idea that every person we encounter is worthy of dignity and respect because every person is made in the image of God. We integrate this radical-embrace perspective

---

[5]We have been influenced by the ideas of Miroslav Volf, particularly his book *Exclusion and Embrace: A Theological Exploration of Identity, Otherness, and Reconciliation* (Nashville: Abingdon, 1996).

throughout the book, showing how this core truth demands different practices and ways of expressing our faith in the workplace.

To be clear, we are not advocating a watered-down Christianity that sees itself as no different from any other religion, nor are we primarily concerned with evaluating the truth claims of other faith traditions. Rather, we are arguing for the equivalent value and dignity of each person and for an approach to Christianity in the workplace that recognizes and centers on such.

The cultural shifts we described at the beginning of this chapter are already underway. How we respond to these shifts will determine whether faith at work retreats into a self-protective corner or becomes a redemptive presence with ripple effects for the common good far beyond its immediate reach. Using compelling real-world stories, research insights, and practical applications, we hope to provide new information, ideas, and guidance for Christian workers, Christian workplace leaders, and pastors and church leaders who want to see all people flourish at work. We close each chapter with questions that can be used for personal reflection or group discussion. Our primary goal is to help those in the Christian faith community consider how to adapt their approach to a changing world in which older ways can get in the way and newer ways open the way.

REFLECTION QUESTIONS

For everyone

- What messages have you heard about integrating faith and work?
- What made you pick up this book? What do you want to get out of this book?
- What are your fears about integrating faith and work in your workplace or particular job?
- What are the challenges for integrating faith and work in your workplace?

For faith communities

- What is the approach of your church or faith-based organization to helping people integrate faith and work?
- What changes would you like your church or faith-based organization to make related to engaging faith at work? Why? What is at stake with these changes?

2

SECULAR WORK

So I hated life, because the work that is done under the sun was grievous to me. All of it is meaningless, a chasing after the wind.

ECCLESIASTES 2:17

CARMY BERZATTO STRUGGLES with the transition from being a chef in high-end fine dining to running his family's sandwich shop in the show *The Bear*. In a moment of raw frustration and exhaustion, he says, "I feel like I'm trying to fix everything all the time, but nothing gets better. It just keeps getting worse." His passion for cooking, combined with the burden of managing a family business, feels like an endless cycle of trying and failing, leaving him feeling stuck despite his talent and effort.

Movies and literature are replete with examples of people who are doing work that lacks fulfillment in spite of their best efforts. This is not new; the Old Testament writer of Ecclesiastes complains about the lack of meaning he observes in all the "work that is done under the sun." One response to this experience of meaninglessness is to separate our work from the rest of our lives. If we can think of work as something that is not really part of what is most important for us, perhaps we can avoid this lack of meaning.

VIEWING WORK AS SECULAR

When we tell other academic social scientists that we have spent the past twenty years studying faith in workplaces (including, for Elaine, scientific workplaces, a context that most think ought to be the most secular), many ask, "Why would you do that? What place does religion have at work?" There are often good reasons for holding this view, since faith can be a divisive force. For many of us, it makes sense to see work as completely secular so that we can bracket it off from things that have more meaning and purpose.[1] Some people may think of work as generally secular because it is not viewed as a place where the focus is primarily on God. Christians who hold this view of work as separate from faith may do so because they want to put most of their energy into pursuits outside work that are more obviously filled with intrinsic meaning for them. As one bivocational pastor who works as a truck driver during the week put it, "The purpose of the workplace is to make money. . . . The church is the place to worship and express your faith."[2]

Faith-at-work expert Jeff Haanen says that secularity happens in two ways. First is what philosopher Charles Taylor calls "exclusive humanism," in which the world excludes any explanation of reality that is not built around humans or human action.[3] It is easy for Christians to reject this type of secularity, as it is obviously and directly opposed to a belief in God. A second way secularism occurs is more like polytheism, the belief that there are many gods. We think theologian Lesslie Newbigin has the right angle on the polytheistic approach to secularity.[4] He argues that while Christians may say that we worship only God, in practice we may be worshiping other gods as well—not necessarily other spiritual beings but workplace idols such as power, prestige,

---

[1]When we say a practice is *secular*, we mean in part that it is not bound by authority of the church or religious leaders.

[2]Faith-at-Work (F@W)_Survey Taker (ST) 48, White man, age 39, pastor/truck driver, evangelical, interview conducted February 5, 2019.

[3]Charles Taylor, *A Secular Age* (Cambridge, MA: Belknap, 2018).

[4]Lesslie Newbigin, *The Gospel in a Pluralist Society* (Grand Rapids, MI: Eerdmans, 1989).

and money, or the desire for security and provision (or even inertia!), which become the primary reasons for our jobs. Thoughtful Christians know at an intellectual level that this polytheistic secularity is counter to God's purposes, but it may be more difficult than exclusive humanism to root out in practice.

We believe that there is a third way in which secularity can gain traction in our lives, and it is this third way to which many Christians seem to default. This is the seemingly benign idea that to be secular is to be related to "worldly concerns," which are generally unimportant in the grand scheme of things, and that work is one of those worldly concerns. In this view work simply has less purchase or concern than those aspects of life that are more obviously spiritual. Yes, we need to work in order to live, but the kind of work we do and even how we do it is not as important as what we do outside the workplace. In some sense, this approach is the exact inverse of the exclusive-humanism approach, and yet its implications are equally problematic.

There has been a significant effort over the past two decades to push back against this way of thinking and to encourage Christians to consider their work as a place where God wants to engage and use them. In the early 2000s, Redeemer Church in New York City started a Center for Faith and Work under the leadership of Katherine Leary Alsdorf, and soon a number of other faith-at-work institutes and centers had sprung up across the country and then around the world.[5] People began to write books on the topic, and a number of fellows programs were initiated, all in an effort to help Christians approach their work as a spiritual endeavor. Several faith-at-work summits were held, and forums and conferences were convened, bringing thousands of people together to explore what the Christian faith might have to say about their work. Denominations began to add workplace ministries in local churches. Yet, in spite of all of the efforts of the faith-at-work movement, the most common opinion is

---

[5]Timothy Keller and Katherine L. Alsdorf, *Every Good Endeavor: Connecting Your Work to God's Work* (New York: Dutton, 2012).

still that faith belongs in sacred settings, such as church and Bible study groups, but has very little to do with the daily activities of work. Most Christians in the United States today continue to view their work and their faith as distinct domains, affected by a long history of thought going back to the ancient Greeks, who created a distinction between the material and the transcendent, with the transcendent being valued above the material. While this sacred-secular divide is not a biblical concept, it has shaped the belief of most Western Christians.[6]

This sacred-secular divide also influences how Christians think about calling. For centuries, Christians have believed that the concept of calling is primarily for those who work in religious settings full time. This idea dates back to the Middle Ages, when the term *calling* was reserved for those who were called by God to become priests, monks, or nuns. These people were special—called by God to do God's work and set apart from the mundane activities of common people doing common work, who did not have such a calling.

We found that many of those we interviewed thought that the types of jobs with the highest potential to serve God included working directly for the church, as a pastor or worship leader, for example, or perhaps being involved directly in Christian ministry through a parachurch organization. One man who works as an engineer told us, "If it comes down to it, a priest or nun or something like that, [perhaps] a deacon, really does the spiritual work. As for me, I see no real connection [to spirituality] . . . as far as my company and my career and my job."[7] The belief this man expressed, that only those who work for the church have a calling, is unfortunate since there are only about 450,000 clergy in the United States, and clergy are disproportionately White and male. The idea that only those who

---

[6]Brenton Kalinowski, Denise Daniels, Rachel C. Schneider, and Elaine Howard Ecklund, "Called to Work: Developing a Framework for Understanding Spiritual Orientations Towards Work," *Sociology of Religion* 85, no. 1 (2023): 1-27.

[7]F@W_ST20, White man, age 50, engineering manager, Catholic, interview conducted November 29, 2018.

work as clergy have a spiritual job or can experience God's calling in their work is severely limiting, since most of those who attend church will never become clergy.

MEANING AND CALLING

Through our surveys we found that only about 20 percent of people in the United States view their work as a spiritual calling. It is worth noting that these numbers are not reflective of Christians specifically but of all workers in the United States. In comparison, 37 percent of evangelical Christians, 25 percent of mainline Christians, and 18 percent of Catholics see their work this way (see fig. 2.1). (We should note that these categories of Christians were determined by both self-description and denominational affiliation.)

Those who agree that their work is a spiritual calling

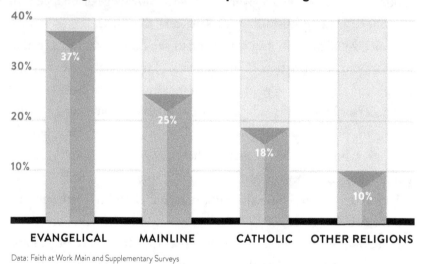

Data: Faith at Work Main and Supplementary Surveys

Figure 2.1

In other words, the large majority of workers do *not* see their jobs as a calling. We have some hunches as to why this might be. Historically, Christians in the West—and, indeed, all of those in the West who have been shaped by Greek philosophy—have bought into the Platonic notion that work, and particularly physical labor, is something to be avoided if possible. This negative view of labor has permeated our view of work more broadly. We also do not often hear pastors talking about work or calling from the pulpit.[8]

Some industries have particularly low levels of workers who feel spiritually called to their work, such as manufacturing (11 percent) and retail sales (13 percent), while other industries—particularly those that involve relational work serving others—have comparatively high rates of workers who feel a sense of calling. These include education (35 percent), caretaking (33 percent), community or social services (33 percent), and health care (28 percent).

Of minds and money. Our research reveals that the notion of work as secular influences those in some professions more than others and that most people view some kinds of work as more spiritual than other kinds. The more aligned a given job is with knowledge or finance professions (e.g., many business roles, sciences), the harder it is for people to conceive of that job as a calling or to see how to do work in that profession in a distinctively Christian way. "I think that some jobs that people can take . . . they're more about making themselves money and not necessarily serving God [laughs]. . . . I think, if you're doing things to help the public, though . . . that's a calling," said a Christian engineer. "Not everybody has that mentality that they want to do that. A lot of people don't like to work with the public, so you have to be kind of called to do that and have the right personality and frame of mind."[9] Notice two things this engineer was saying. First, jobs that are about making money are not a calling, whereas jobs that serve others are. Second, not everyone has the temperament to serve others well. The implicit takeaway from this kind of thinking is that only a few people who have the "right personality and frame of mind" have the

---

[8]Elaine Howard Ecklund, Denise Daniels, and Rachel C. Schneider, "From Secular to Sacred: Bringing Work to Church," *Religions* 11, no. 9 (2020): 442.

[9]F@W_ST39, White woman, age 39, engineer, evangelical, interview conducted January 16, 2019.

opportunity to do jobs that are experienced as a calling. It is particularly notable that this view was expressed by an engineer—someone who did not view her own work as a calling because she did not see it as working with the public.

Both of us have had experiences interacting with people who struggle to see any sense of calling or aspects of faith in their work. One time, after Denise gave a talk on God's purpose for business, a Christian man in the banking industry asked her how his work in the investment world could matter to God. He did not think about how his work was making it possible for people to buy homes, start businesses that make products people need, employ others, and so on. He viewed his work as a way to make money but did not see the potential his work had to be a partnership with God in accomplishing God's purposes in the world. Our research shows that those who agree that the primary reason they work is to make money are less likely to feel a sense of calling in their work (see fig. 2.2).

We have both talked with friends across various occupations who are looking forward to retirement, even

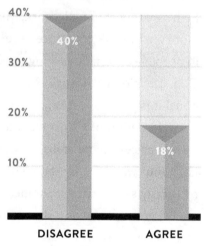

Respondents who see their work as a calling depending on whether they agree or disagree with the statement "The primary reason I work is to make money."

DISAGREE   AGREE

Data: Faith at Work Main and Supplementary Surveys

Figure 2.2

though it might be ten or twenty years away, because they feel retirement will provide space in their lives to finally do work that feels more missional. There is a real and widespread sense that the jobs they have now, and the work they are doing on a daily basis, are simply a way to earn a living. At best, they view their work in a utilitarian way—as a means to an end. Through their work they are able to make money to support their family or do something else that is more important to them. "I've always thought that, you know, maybe at some point in my career, more than likely later in my career, once my children are out and gone and off the payroll, and we're set for retirement, that I would take some time at the end of my career to maybe look at doing something more of what I want to do versus what I have to do," said one man in his fifties who works in industrial sales.[10] A scientist Elaine once interviewed about how his scientific work is connected to his faith as a Christian told her he thinks the primary connection is making money to give to mission work. She could not help but think that there are certainly other ways of making money that are easier than being a scientist!

Care work as spiritual work. A majority of those we talked with as part of our research seemed to have a binary understanding of how faith is connected with work, viewing those jobs that are closer to money as inherently more secular, and those jobs that are closer to people—especially helping people—as more spiritual and closer to God. The closer the work is to a caring profession, or the more relational it is, the easier it is for Christians to see how that work could be a manifestation of Christian convictions. Perhaps part of the reason these service-oriented jobs are viewed as more spiritual is that when it is obvious who is being served by the work, the job becomes more intrinsically satisfying. An engineer explained it this way: "There's definitely more satisfaction doing something, say, with manufacturing pharmaceuticals, which are directly helping people, than working in a plant making paint, right?"[11]

Even in this hierarchy, Christians tend to elevate church jobs above jobs that do not directly serve the church. A grocery store clerk told us that jobs in which people are being helped are the more valuable jobs, but if you have the opportunity to work in the church, that serves God

---

[10]F@W_ST184, White man, age 50, industrial sales, Catholic, interview conducted December 18, 2019.
[11]F@W_ST72, White man, age 23, engineer, Catholic, interview conducted May 19, 2019.

the most.[12] Short of that, any "kind of job where you are helping people" is a more spiritual job, she said.

"I mean, I don't know if you'd really consider what I do serving God," said a delivery truck driver we interviewed, "but I would think, yeah, if you're like a missionary or something, you know, something in the religious field, yeah."[13] A man who works in the finance industry does not see his own work as spiritual but did identify other jobs that he thinks are: "Like a preacher or a pastor . . . they're not only serving God but they're serving people at the same time. They are serving their parishioners in translating . . . the Word of God to them. . . . Parishioners are able to understand and have their faith and grow their faith. So that's a valuable job."[14] He went on to talk about firefighters and police officers, who are not ranked as highly as clergy in his hierarchy of calling, yet he sees these jobs as rewarding because they serve people. Outside clergy, he views being a teacher as perhaps the highest spiritual calling because teachers serve so many kids. In contrast, he had quite a negative view of those doing more menial tasks: "I would be fearful if somebody felt like they were doing the Lord's work handing somebody a cup of coffee," he concluded. "You know, it's just not the same. It is not the same."

Even those who are not part of the Christian tradition tend to think work that helps others directly is both more spiritual and, hence more valuable than work that does not have this direct interpersonal interaction. For example, a practicing Muslim who works as part of the technical staff in a for-profit company explained:

> Certainly, I would say . . . being a doctor is a more appealing job, in terms of serving humanity, and, for example, working for nonprofit organizations, working for organizations helping people, wherever that may be. So, that could be nonprofit, it could be NGOs [nongovernmental organizations]. It

---

[12]F@W_ST132, White woman, age 58, scan clerk (grocery store), evangelical, interview conducted September 9, 2019.

[13]F@W_ST51, White man, age 32, delivery truck driver, mainline, interview conducted February 8, 2019.

[14]F@W_ST25, Hispanic man, age 36, asset manager, Catholic, interview conducted December 7, 2018.

could be education as well. I do see those being higher in value [spiritually] than other types of jobs.[15]

Among those Christians we interviewed, there was a consistent lack of imagination for how their jobs could be viewed as in any way connected to their faith. This was true even when the jobs at least indirectly served others and helped people. For example, a university student we interviewed who is working part time on the business side of a hospital thought that the jobs that had "a lot more hands-on interaction with the patients" were more valuable than his.[16] In particular, he singled out those who are there for patients "when they are suffering and when they pass," "like the doctors and nurses," as those who are doing truly spiritual work. Even though he is doing important work and "helping the mission," he believes people in jobs like his, who are working more behind the scenes, are not doing work that is as meaningful.

A privilege of the privileged. It was often especially hard for working-class individuals to see how the kinds of jobs they did served God. We found that those in blue-collar work, in entry-level service jobs, or engaged in the freelance ("gig") economy often have difficulty viewing their work as more than a means of making money or imagining how their work matters to God.[17] From their vantage point, it is hard to see how a person can be empowered through work to bring positive changes to the workplace or the larger world. There can be structural, cultural, or financial factors that restrict a person's ability to pursue a job that is viewed as meaningful or experienced as a calling.

Many of us have been shaped by our culture to minimize the value of some kinds of work, and this translates into how we understand the

---

[15]F@W_ST148, Asian man, age 42, technical staff, Muslim, interview conducted October 17, 2019.

[16]F@W_ST85, Asian man, age 22, student, Catholic, interview conducted June 13, 2019.

[17]See further "Plight of the Blue Collar," Faith and Co., https://faithandco.spu.edu/plight-of-the-blue-collar/, for some excellent resources about faith in the workplaces that include a diversity of types of work. In general, the faith-at-work movement has been very slow to attend to blue-collar jobs.

spiritual meaning of work. Elaine remembers the choir director at the church she grew up in; he seemed larger than life to her child eyes, to have so much power in the congregation as he moved his hands, and voices making beautiful sounds responded in unison. She was incredibly surprised one day when, driving around the neighborhood with her grandmother, she saw him get out of a washing machine repair truck. Her image of this man as being powerful was blown. She remembers her grandmother saying that this was "his day job so he could feed his family and do the work of the Lord for the church on the weekends." Neither she nor her grandmother had the tools from their congregation to imagine how this man could be serving God through his work as a washing machine repairman.

Our research shows that the experience of calling is often perceived to be a privilege of the privileged. Outside professional jobs that focus on helping others, many view only jobs with high levels of power or high responsibility as ones to which it is possible to be called. Figuring out whether one job is more spiritually valuable than another "depends on the level that you're at," a middle-aged Christian man who works as a program manager told us.[18] In his sense of things, those in jobs where they have more power and agency may also have a chance to do things to support ministry, even from within their corporate jobs. Those who have "reached a certain level," he said, "they can have a little bit more influence where you can guide funds, maybe influence the charitable giving that a company does back out to the community, and think you may have more of an impact there."

This perception that those at the top of the organization are more likely to have a calling was not simply a function of outsiders looking in. We found self-assessments of calling to be consistent with this notion that those who are more influential in the organization are more likely to feel they have a calling. People at the top of their organizations

---

[18]F@W_ST09, Black man, age 50, program manager, evangelical, interview conducted November 2, 2018.

are more likely to agree that their work is a spiritual calling than those at the bottom of their organizations (26 percent vs. 16 percent).[19] Those who view their work as a calling are most likely to be in senior-level roles in their organizations. There are a couple of plausible reasons for this. While being at the top of an organization might help foster a sense of calling, it could also be that individuals who feel called to their work tend to move up to the top of an organization.[20] Under certain conditions, it could also be a function of maturity, bringing more thoughtful reflection (although we want to be careful not to assume here that those at the top of an organization are the wisest, while those at the bottom of the organization are less so). Often inequality factors are at play as well.

In what might appear to be a contradiction, we also found that workers who make less money are more likely to see their work as a calling than are those who report higher incomes. For instance, workers with annual household incomes under $89,000 were more likely to see their work as a calling (22 percent) than were those with household incomes of $180,000 or more (17 percent). It may be that the kinds of jobs, roles, or industries in which people are likely to have the highest incomes are also those that align less with people's intuitive sense of meaningful jobs (i.e., those that serve others directly).

These findings may also reflect a difference between those who work in for-profit settings (where a high organizational level is likely to correlate with a high income) and those who work in nonprofit settings (where a high organizational level is less likely to correlate with a high income, but employees are more likely to see their work as a calling). When we look at workers in different sectors, we find that about

---

[19]Survey respondents were asked, "Think about the organization of job roles in your industry, where the leaders are at the top of the organization and employees are at the bottom of the organization. Would you say that you are toward the top of the organization, middle, or at the bottom?" The cross-tabulation of this question with the calling question is statistically significant at $p < 0.001$ (design-based F test).

[20]Kalinowski et al. "Called to Work."

14 percent of workers in the for-profit sector feel spiritually called to their work compared with 36 percent of those in the nonprofit sector.[21]

There is research that can help us understand why those who work in the nonprofit sector experience higher levels of spiritual calling, specifically Edward Deci's work on the over-justification effect. Deci, an organizational psychologist, found that the more people are paid for a task they enjoy, the more they tend to minimize the intrinsic motivation for that task. "It appears that money—perhaps because of its connotation and use in our culture—may act as a stimulus, which leads the [research] subjects to a cognitive reevaluation of the activity from one which is intrinsically motivated to one which is motivated primarily by the expectation of financial rewards," he writes in one study. "In short, money may work to 'buy off' one's intrinsic motivation for an activity. And this decreased motivation appears, (from the results of the field experiment), to be more than just a temporary phenomenon."[22] Think about the kinds of tasks that you might be willing to do when volunteering for a good cause that you would not be excited to do as part of a paid job. For example, many Christians engage in mission trips where they do manual labor to build houses, churches, or wells for those in other countries, but many of those same people would not consider pursuing that same kind of work for paid employment upon their return. (In some sense we experience more meaning in a job with low or no compensation compared with a job where we are well paid.) So, while it could be that individuals who follow their calling are more likely to find themselves in nonprofit jobs where their work centers on helping others and fulfilling a meaningful purpose, or that workers who make less money ascribe a sense of calling to their work to make

---

[21] Percentages represent those who somewhat and strongly agree with the statement "I see my work as a spiritual calling." The cross-tabulation indicates overall significant differences in agreement across work sector types (design-based F test = 30.93, $p < 0.001$).

[22] Edward L. Deci, "Effects of Externally Mediated Rewards on Intrinsic Motivation," *Journal of Personality and Social Psychology* 18 (1971): 105-15; Edward L. Deci, Richard Koestner, and Richard M. Ryan, "A Meta-analytic Review of Experiments Examining the Effects of Extrinsic Rewards on Intrinsic Motivation," *Psychological Bulletin* 125, no. 6 (1999): 627-68.

up for lower compensation, it could also be that workers lose the feeling that their work is a calling the more money they make.

Those who see their work as a calling also tend to feel their work is important beyond making money—thinking more about achieving personal fulfillment and making a difference in the world through their work.[23] In responding to the statement, "The primary reason I work is to make money," fewer than half of people (47 percent) who viewed their work as a spiritual calling agreed, compared with 68 percent of those who do not feel called to their work. So, while making money and having a sense of calling are not mutually exclusive, there does seem to be a tension there, with a focus on making money associated with a lower likelihood of viewing work as a calling and vice versa.

MORE AND LESS SPIRITUAL ASPECTS OF JOBS

In every job, there are some aspects that are positive and, even in the best of jobs, aspects that are difficult, mundane, or menial. Here are the kinds of things we heard from people: "I feel like I am serving God when I am caring for students, but compliance with state-mandated standards seems meaningless." "I love envisioning the big picture of my job as a CEO but can't stand getting in the weeds of the administrative work." "I really appreciate the spiritual impact of helping keep others away from germs through providing a clean room, but the punching in and out on the clock seems to have little purpose." We found that there are *aspects of jobs* that are deemed more spiritual than other aspects.

Our interviews with workers in a variety of jobs revealed that the parts of jobs that are more administrative (think about the classic "paper pushing" or writing endless emails) seem more secular and less meaningful, while the aspects of jobs that are geared more toward one-on-one personal relationships (the aspects of jobs that "help people," as many of our respondents said) are deemed more spiritual and aligned

---

[23]This cross-tabulation is statistically significant at $p < 0.001$ (design-based F test).

with calling. A librarian said it is the aspects of jobs that are more directly related to service that are "probably more valuable work," while a wedding coordinator said it is the aspects of "jobs that give you more of an opportunity to actually interact with people. You know, [those are the more spiritual] if you're getting more of an opportunity to touch people."[24] The CFO of a credit union told us: "Maybe some [aspects of] jobs have more potential impact because . . . they're interfacing, interacting with more people. . . . Maybe you just interact with just a handful of people, whereas you could have somebody like a teller at a branch, you're meeting a lot more people and so you have a lot more opportunity to interact with people that way," even though there are other aspects of being a teller that involve simply counting money.[25]

The workers we talked with were aware of the aspects of their jobs they see as meaningful and aligned with their perceptions of calling as well as those aspects that are less meaningful and less aligned with their perceptions of calling. Rarely, however, do they have the agency or tools to change the aspects of their jobs they feel are less important or to spend more time doing what they see as the spiritual aspects of their jobs.

JOBS WITH NO REDEMPTIVE POSSIBILITIES

There are some jobs that workers see as having no potential at all to serve God and as explicitly counter to Christian teachings, and in our research Christian workers are very clear on what sorts of jobs these are. It was not surprising to us that those we interviewed mentioned jobs in bars and strip clubs—which involve tobacco and alcohol or what they see as sinful use of sexuality—as those that have no possibility for spiritual influence. Some even said these jobs are "evil."

---

[24]F@W_ST52, White woman, age 64, librarian, mainline, interview conducted February 12, 2019; F@W_ST60, White woman, age 53, wedding coordinator, evangelical, interview conducted February 28, 2019.

[25]F@W_ST10, White man, age 59, CFO of credit union, evangelical, interview conducted November 6, 2018.

A man who manages a logging company said straightforwardly, "There are some jobs that I think do not honor and glorify God."[26] As he started listing these jobs, he said he would not be "involved . . . in the alcohol or tobacco industry . . . and I'm not saying that it's wrong to use alcohol at all. . . . But there is nothing about tobacco . . . that is a benefit. But I would say that the Bible does talk about the use of alcohol, at least medicinally, as being appropriate, and most people don't use it that way, so therefore I would not be involved in—in producing it."

A graphic artist told us that he has "made a conscious choice not to take jobs that would violate certain biblical principles, or things that I don't think would be honoring to God. So, you know, I've had offers to do logos for strip clubs, and I told them I can't do it. I've had people try to hire me to design logos for pot dispensaries, and I've told them . . . I can't do that [laughs]."[27] He has questions that help him make these decisions, he said: "God gave me these talents, what am I using them for? Would he be pleased with the things that I'm promoting with my skills, or would he be displeased? And I use that as a guide." A woman who works as a caretaker said, "If you are going to work at a bar," then "that would have nothing to do with faith and would hence not be a job that honors God."[28]

Those we interviewed thought people who work in jobs that "chase money" have minimal or no spiritual influence; they had little vision for how these kinds of jobs could be spiritual. According to a reimbursement analyst: "I do believe that there are positions where people are able to serve God with their approach to life. . . . I think a job such as teaching and counseling and stuff like that is kind of . . . more lined up with God's will. But not my job, where my main purpose is to make sure that the doctor I work for simply gets the amount of money he

---

[26]F@W_ST33, White man, age 48, co-owner of logging company, evangelical, interview conducted January 8, 2019.
[27]F@W_ST43, Black man, age 48, graphic artist, evangelical, interview conducted January 29, 2019.
[28]F@W_ST120, Hispanic woman, age 48, caretaker, Catholic, interview conducted August 29, 2019.

should get [laughs]."[29] Workers we interviewed also said that jobs do not serve God if they take an individual away from church. For example, a woman who packs flour that is used to manufacture bread told us that a job is less valuable or even sinful if it leads you away from God.[30] She said that at one point she had a job with a very good salary, earning more than she does now, but she was "unable to go to church." Because she felt the job was taking her away from God, she decided to switch to a lower-paying job that allows her more time to participate in her congregation.

PUTTING LIMITS ON WORK

We will spend a lot of time critiquing the view that work is secular, and we ourselves align heavily with the view that most work can be redeemed. In the next chapter, we will examine ways to diminish the sacred-secular divide between work and worship.

But there is one way in which seeing work as secular might have a positive effect. We want you to slow down here and take in the possibility that there can be a danger in viewing one's work as sacred: our work can feel so meaningful and important that it inadvertently becomes an idol, something that is more important to us than even God, and we can come to see our work for pay as the most important and potentially only kind of calling we have.

There are many examples of individuals who have elevated their work above all else and ultimately failed at the other important things in life. We can readily point to movie stars, political leaders, Fortune 500 CEOs—and sometimes even pastors—whose skills are admired and revered by many, yet who have wrecked their marriages or have children who do not speak to them because they have given everything to their work. It is common to hear the advice that work should take a

---

[29]F@W_ST71, Black woman, age 66, reimbursement analyst, evangelical, interview conducted May 28, 2019.

[30]F@W_ST135, Hispanic woman, age 27, packer, evangelical, interview conducted September 17, 2019.

back seat to other demands in life: "When you are on your deathbed, you aren't going to wish you'd put in more time at the office," the expression goes. Putting all of our hope, meaning, and purpose into our work can lead to depression and even death, hence the saying, "He worked himself to death!" A social-scientific sidenote on the gendered pronoun here: Research shows that, historically, men, particularly those who had high-powered jobs, have been much more likely than women to experience depression or even die shortly after they retired because they had little outside of work that gave them true meaning. Researchers have hypothesized that one of the reasons women often have better health outcomes than men in retirement is that they are more likely to have meaningful pursuits outside their work. Friendships and family relationships, which women are socialized to value, turn out to be associated with better mental and physical health and longevity. Yet, recent increases in US death rates for women are attributed by some researchers to be the result of more women moving into the kinds of high-powered, identity-totalizing careers that until recently have been occupied mainly by men.[31]

Professionals often spend most of their waking hours at work and many of the remaining hours thinking about work. Our research shows that it is especially challenging to put limits on work that is connected to helping people (such as medical work, teaching, or social work). It is also hard to put limits on work when you are part of an industry that sees long hours as a badge of honor, such as medicine, the tech and legal industries, or academic work in universities. Workplaces and different job types often have cultures that we begin to embody without having space to think about it. In our quest to show the limits of seeing work as secular, we do not want to inadvertently advocate a perspective that sees all of life as work. We need to ask ourselves, "What is work doing to me?"

[31]See in particular Marianne Gjellestad, Kristin Haraldstad, Heidi Enehaug, and Migle Helmersen, "Women's Health and Working Life: A Scoping Review," *International Journal of Environmental Research and Public Health* 20, no. 2 (2023): 1080.

REFLECTION QUESTIONS

For everyone

- Reflect on the tasks of your job. Which aspects of your work do you see as most secular and which as most sacred? Why?

- What aspects of your work would be most difficult to integrate with your faith?

- In your view, what is calling? To what extent is calling more dependent on the person, and to what extent is calling more dependent on the particular job? How do you see the tension between these?

- In your particular work role, to what extent do you think that there might be a downside to the view that your work can be sacred?

For faith communities

- What kind of opportunities are you providing for people in your church or organization to integrate faith and work?

- What kinds of resources for integrating faith and work have you been using? What has been lacking in those resources?

3

SACRED WORK

Whatever you do, work at it with all your heart, as
working for the Lord, not for human masters, since you
know that you will receive an inheritance from the Lord
as a reward. It is the Lord Christ you are serving.

COLOSSIANS 3:23-24

KRISTA IS A DOCTORAL STUDENT in marine biology trying to understand and implement difficult molecular heating processes.[1] Our interview with Krista had a special impact on us; she seemed to say things related to multiple themes that emerged in our research. So, we decided to give her a pseudonym and come back to her a couple of times in the book. (For similar reasons we will occasionally use names for other interview respondents.)

Krista sometimes spends two weeks to a month out at sea, away from her family and friends. Some of the professors she has worked with throughout her career have been so terrific that they inspired her and helped her realize that "I would love to be in a role where I can share what I'm passionate about with others and help students possibly find

---

[1]F@W_ST99, White/Hispanic woman, age 23, PhD student in marine biology, evangelical, interview conducted July 12, 2019.

what they are passionate about, to have opportunities to mentor students at a very important time in their lives." But she has noticed that other scientists who lead large research groups often seem to care more about themselves than the next generation of scientists, and she finds the competitive culture of science and the power hierarchies she must navigate difficult, not to mention the profession's approach to religion.[2] Sometimes—because of her faith—she feels belittled by other scientists at work.

Krista's view of her scientific work is deeply informed by Christian values that compel her to act against the prevailing norms of self-interest that she commonly encounters in science. "I think that all truth is from God, and as a scientist, I try to understand and reveal the truth of how the world works, and so in that sense my calling is a spiritual calling," she said. This feeling of being spiritually called to her work helps Krista overcome some of its challenges, gives her a higher purpose, keeps her motivated to do the best science she can, and leads her to think strategically about how to help others through her work. "Calling is everything," she said. "I wouldn't stay if I didn't feel called."

In this chapter we talk about what it means to view work as sacred. We provide data from our research that shows the conditions under which people view their work as sacred, and what types of jobs and work tasks are most likely to be viewed as sacred. We also provide the practical help of Scripture, Christian teaching, and lessons (both good and bad!) from our own lives.

The writer of Romans says, "Do not conform to the *pattern* of this world" (Romans 12:2). The word *pattern* connotes thinking and doing certain things that are like the things those in the world around us do and think. As Christians, we are to discern in community with other followers of the faith what the patterns of this world are and how we

---

[2]See Elaine Howard Ecklund and Anne E. Lincoln, *Failing Families, Failing Science: Work-Family Conflict in Academic Science* (New York: New York University Press, 2016).

might have renewed minds and practices that help us do our work—which might take a variety of forms, even within a particular job. First, we will look at the different ways that Christians we surveyed and interviewed understand their work to be sacred and have sacred aspects, integrating their work and faith. Then we will explore what we see as missed opportunities for Christians to view certain aspects of their work as more sacred, suggesting some very practical ways that workers in virtually any job might find meaning in their work, improve their experience of work, positively influence their workplace or those they work with, and pursue the common good.

BEING CALLED

In the present day, the concept of calling, introduced earlier, is the most prominent way that those we surveyed and interviewed saw the sacred aspects of their work or how their work connected to their faith. Not all who see their work as a calling describe it in religious terms, although, due to the history of calling, it is a concept more popular among Christians. As we briefly discussed in the last chapter, calling during the Middle Ages referred to a call from God to the monastic life. If you had a call from God, or a vocation (the Latin *vocatio* is translated as "calling" in English), you gave up your regular, secular life and moved to a monastery, where you would pursue a sacred life in stark contrast to the run-of-the-mill work that most people did.

The perspective on calling changed dramatically in the mid-1500s with the Protestant Reformation. Theologian and reformer Martin Luther pushed back against the concept of calling as accessible only to some and applied only to full-time Christian ministry. He believed that all types of work could be a calling from God, developing this idea from 1 Corinthians 7:17, which says, "Each person should live as a believer in whatever situation the Lord has assigned to them." In his view, all legitimate work—in other words, work that is not illegal or immoral—has equal spiritual dignity and is a form of serving God and accomplishing God's purposes on earth.[3] Luther's perspective was so strong that he actually elevated mundane work above a monastic call. "It looks like a small thing when a maid cooks and cleans and does other housework," he writes, but such work "far surpass[es] the holiness and asceticism of all monks and nuns."[4]

The Puritans carried this Reformation notion of work as calling even further. They indicated two types of calling that each of us have: a general call and a specific call. The general call is the summons from God to be in relationship with God. This type of calling is reflected in a famous statement widely attributed to Mother Teresa: "God has not called me to be successful. He has called me to be faithful." But Puritans also believed that God called people to be successful. This type of calling is what they referred to as a specific call, and it involves all the jobs and tasks particular to each person that are done in service to God and others. While this specific call might include one's paid work, it goes far beyond a job to include a person's responsibilities to their family and friends, and their roles within their Christian community and larger society. Our research reveals that this revisioning of all of life as calling has not widely permeated the everyday work lives of most American Christians, who still tend to connect spiritual calling with working for the church in some way. But we did catch glimpses of these varied concepts of calling.

FOUR WAYS TO UNDERSTAND CALLING

As we talked with workers, we found they tended to describe their experience of calling in some consistent categories. We have created a framework with two dimensions to help explain these distinct ways of understanding work as calling (see fig. 3.1). The horizontal dimension of this framework focuses on whether an individual experiences

[3]Adriano Tilgher, *Work: What It Has Meant to Men Through the Ages*, trans. Dorothy Canfield Fisher (New York: Harcourt Brace, 1930), 49.

[4]Martin Luther, *Luther's Works*, American ed. (St. Louis: Concordia, 1967), 5:102.

purpose or meaning in the work itself. If someone finds meaning due to the direct substance of the work they do, we identify that as an *intrinsic orientation to work*. On the other hand, someone might find meaning indirectly through their work. Whether or not the work itself seems meaningful, it provides purpose and meaning that they would not otherwise have. In some sense, the work is a means to an end. We call this an *extrinsic orientation to work*.

The vertical dimension of our framework is concerned with whether a worker has an orientation toward seeing and experiencing God's purposes *within the workplace* itself, or whether they see and experience God's purposes in how aspects of the work affect individuals or communities *beyond the workplace*. This can be thought of as a *location of service* dimension, where some workers focus on the impact of their work very near to where the work is being done, and others are looking for an impact further away from the work itself. When these two dimensions are combined, they create a model with four quadrants.

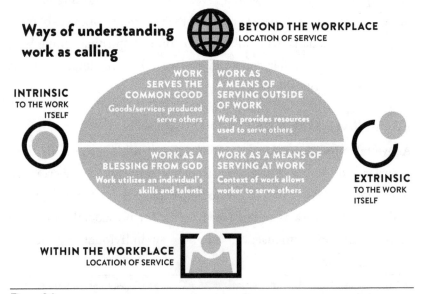

Ways of understanding work as calling

BEYOND THE WORKPLACE
LOCATION OF SERVICE

INTRINSIC
TO THE WORK
ITSELF

WORK SERVES THE COMMON GOOD
Goods/services produced serve others

WORK AS A MEANS OF SERVING OUTSIDE OF WORK
Work provides resources used to serve others

WORK AS A BLESSING FROM GOD
Work utilizes an individual's skills and talents

WORK AS A MEANS OF SERVING AT WORK
Context of work allows worker to serve others

EXTRINSIC
TO THE WORK
ITSELF

WITHIN THE WORKPLACE
LOCATION OF SERVICE

Figure 3.1

It is important to note that these four quadrants are not mutually exclusive. These dimensions are not meant to categorize individuals but rather are different ways of viewing work as a calling. Those who see their work as a calling will often express perspectives that reflect multiple aspects of the framework.[5] Indeed, it is possible—and beneficial!—to locate one's understanding of one's work in *each* of the four quadrants. At the same time, many of the people we spoke with tended toward having one or two quadrants dominate their perception of their work as calling.

Intrinsic/within the workplace: Work as a blessing from God. The intrinsic/within orientation toward work as a calling sees the work being done as intrinsically important or good, and the impact of that goodness is very close to the worker, either within the immediate workplace environment or even within the individual doing the work. Work is seen as a calling because the work itself is meaningful, and workers see themselves as aligning with the mission or purpose of their specific workplace. They may see the work they do as meeting personal goals, such as professionalization or contentment, and they see a strong match between the demands of the work and their own talents and interests.

Viewing their work through this lens, individuals see the skills used to do their job as a gift from God, or they believe they have been given the opportunity to do their job as a blessing from God—and as evidence of their calling to their work. Those we interviewed frequently shared this perspective, discussing skills or interests they have that align with specific types of work or the demands of their job. We would hear people say things like, "I was made to do this work," or "God guided me to this exact job." A man who works in human resources and considers his work a spiritual calling told us his job is a good use of his math skill set, which is an indication that he has found his calling and

---

[5]Calling was not always understood in the same way for people of different religions, and other religious concepts were sometimes more pertinent for Jewish and Muslim individuals when discussing meaning and work.

is fulfilling God's purposes through his job.[6] "We should pray and really ask God, 'What is our purpose? How does our secular job line up to what God has for our life?'" he said, "and I really do believe that I've been really good with numbers and math ever since I was in high school."

Other workers said that God gave them specific gifts or virtues, such as patience or the ability to serve others, that they use to glorify God through their work. "I truly believe that the Lord has built me with the ability to work with difficult people, to have a clear head when things are going really bad . . . and I'm doing the Lord's work," a corrections officer told us.[7] "And how can you go wrong by doing the Lord's work?" This idea of doing the Lord's work is another way of understanding one's work as being approved by God. For workers with an intrinsic/within orientation toward work as a calling, finding their calling and where they fit in God's plan also means understanding and doing what God desires.

Intrinsic/beyond the workplace: Work serves the common good. Those with an intrinsic/beyond orientation to work as a calling view their work as having value because what is being created or accomplished through the work is intrinsically important, and the work's impact is located outside the workplace. This view can overlap with the idea of receiving gifts from God, but the emphasis is on the idea that the work has meaning beyond the individual doing the work, and the impact of the work is felt beyond the workplace.[8] Much of the current faith-at-work movement is focused on helping people expand their perception of the ways in which the work they do is intrinsically meaningful with impact beyond themselves, and this approach aligns well with this quadrant of the framework.

[6]F@W_ST73, Black man, age 31, human resources, evangelical, interview conducted May 9, 2019.
[7]F@W_ST11, White man, age 63, corrections officer, evangelical, interview conducted November 8, 2018.
[8]Brenton Kalinowski, Denise Daniels, Rachel C. Schneider, and Elaine Howard Ecklund, "Called to Work: Developing a Framework for Understanding Spiritual Orientations Towards Work," *Sociology of Religion* 85, no. 1 (2023): 1-27. Some of the points in this chapter are also discussed in this article.

Often, responses that fit in this category came from those who see their work as meaningful because they can benefit broader society with the goods or services that they or their organization provide. While helping individuals face to face might be part of these individuals' work, they see the ultimate good of their work applying on a larger scale, whether that be their local community, the country, or all of humanity. Although we heard this view of calling most commonly from those working in fields focused on caring for others, such as medicine or social service, workers in a variety of fields, including engineering, science, and food services, expressed an intrinsic/beyond orientation in their view of work as a calling. This framing was less likely from those who worked in entry-level service jobs or in blue-collar kinds of work. It was not as common for these people to focus on the ways in which their work was intrinsically meaningful or affected others beyond the workplace. Yet we did hear this common-good perspective across a number of different roles and industries.

For example, a woman who works as an engineer designing city water systems views her work as a calling because through her work she can ensure her whole city is supplied with safe water.[9] Another woman who works in political fundraising sees her work as contributing to flourishing on a national scale, though she admits that not everyone would view it that way.[10] "I do think it is a spiritual calling for me," she said.

> I love politics, and I think there's a need for politics, and I do feel like the work I'm doing is helping to change the world, and I know half the population doesn't agree with me just because of the party I represent, but I do feel like the party that I represent helps Americans live better and their policies overall help change the lives of Americans, and I believe in that. I mean, I do think it's my calling because not a lot of people want to do politics or work in fundraising, but it's necessary.

---

[9]F@W_ST39, White woman, age 39, engineer, evangelical, interview conducted January 16, 2019.
[10]F@W_ST172, White woman, age 26, account executive in political fundraising, evangelical, interview conducted December 9, 2019.

For individuals who see the benefit of their work outside their work-place, it was most common for them to view the impact as still somewhat local, benefiting a particular group of people in a particular community. Only a very small number are able to see their work as positively contributing to the country or the entire world. Krista, the student in marine biology we met at the beginning of the chapter, sees the knowledge she gains through her work as having this kind of broader impact.[11] "I think that all truth is from God, and as a scientist I pursue and I try to understand and reveal truth of how the world works," she said, "and so in that sense I think that is a spiritual calling because I am totally understanding how the world was created and bringing truth to light."

For some individuals, working at a company that provides a product they see as benefiting society is a calling, even if their particular piece of the actual work is mundane or extremely stressful. They recognize the broader impact of the larger workplace of which they are a part, viewing their work as a way they can serve others even if their role is removed from those who are directly benefiting. "When I do accept a role, I definitely take into consideration the level of good I perceive [the company] does," said a man who works in the corporate offices of a global fast-food restaurant that he considers a healthier food alternative for people around the world.[12] "The fact that . . . [this company pro-vides] vegetables and food that people can conceivably be nourished by, and located in some of the toughest regions in the world, and they feed a lot of people every day, I definitely considered, does that line up with what I'm called upon to do by the Gospels?"

Extrinsic/beyond the work: Work as means of serving outside work. In the extrinsic/beyond orientation to work as a calling, the meaning

---

[11]F@W_ST99, White/Hispanic woman, age 23, PhD student in marine biology, evangelical, inter-view conducted July 12, 2019.
[12]F@W_ST12, Hispanic man, age 33, external communications manager, evangelical, interview conducted November 14, 2018.

of work is extraneous to the nature of the work itself and not specifically related to the goods or services being provided. Unlike the intrinsic/beyond orientation, this view does not focus on the benefit to others as derived from the specific tasks or outcomes of the work itself. Rather, in this quadrant the focus is on how the skills or benefits gained through the work allow people to find meaning outside the workplace. For many who express this view, their work is a means to an end, providing them with the abilities or resources to serve others outside work, typically those with whom they have personal relationships, such as their family, their immediate religious community, or other community members. Individuals we spoke with whose approach to work fits in this category sometimes did physically demanding work. "It's supportive of my spiritual calling. . . . It provides the funds so that I can do what I believe I need to do," the co-owner of a logging company said of his work and the financial means it provides to help others and attend to his spiritual calling.[13] "It is to bring honor and glory to God, in any way possible. If that is witnessing to a neighbor, if that is helping someone who has financial, mental, spiritual difficulties, health issues, I see it to bring honor and glory to God."

From others we interviewed, too, we heard comments that reminded us of using one's work to fulfill the Puritans' notion of specific calling, which includes roles a person might fill within their family and community. The most common example of this kind of specific calling we heard involved caring for family. As one engineer told us, "My work is more of a calling to support my primary vocation, which is getting married and raising a family."[14] These ideas had resonance with those outside Christian communities. When asked whether she viewed her work as a spiritual calling, a Jewish woman who works as an EMT and freelance writer focused not on how her work as an EMT was fulfilling

---

[13]F@W_ST33, White man, age 48, co-owner of logging company, evangelical, interview conducted January 8, 2019.

[14]F@W_ST72, White man, age 23, engineer, Catholic, interview conducted May 19, 2019.

or meaningful or how it directly helped people, but rather on how her work allows her to care for her family.[15] "The way we look at it is that your intentions matter a lot. . . . If your intention is also to support your family, then it becomes a spiritual pursuit because your kids need to eat. Your kids need shoes. Your kids need school supplies. You need a roof over your head," she said. "There's no real separation between what you're calling spiritual when you have the right intentions. So, as far as working to support my family, that's an overall yes."

A woman who works in marketing replied to the idea of her work being a calling by saying, "My job now pays the bills, it allows me flexibility, it allows me to work from home at times, and just [the] ability to kind of have my family be my main ministry."[16] While she spoke of her current job in these extrinsic/beyond terms, she spoke about her previous job at a women's shelter as being a calling in an intrinsic/beyond way, where she saw the impact of her work on the larger community through the services her shelter provided. When she changed jobs, the way she viewed her job as a calling also changed. This reveals that viewing work as a calling is a subjective and interpretive process, and an individual's perception of their work can change over time. This often happens when we change what we do for our work, but it could also happen within the same job.

Several other workers we spoke with focused on how they use resources or skills gained at work to serve their faith community. "Is the work that I do at this company a spiritual calling? No," a person who works in information technology told us.[17] "Is learning what I learned from doing, maintaining those skills, and continuing those skills, do I see that as a spiritual calling? Well, it seems like it to me because I use

---

[15]F@W_ST122, White woman, age 34, freelance writer and EMT, Jewish, interview conducted August 30, 2019.

[16]F@W_ST104, White, woman, age 31, director of partner marketing, evangelical, interview conducted July 25, 2019.

[17]F@W_ST174, White man, age 35, IT associate, evangelical, interview conducted December 10, 2019.

those skills to help the ministry whenever and wherever possible. People from ministries will call for tech support. I just help them. I don't charge." In other words, his work allows him to develop skills, and he uses these skills to fulfill a calling to serve the church. Like many other Christian workers in our research, he identifies serving the church as the best and highest calling one can have. "Our gifts are for the church, and we're allowed to use and strengthen them outside of the church, but the gifts themselves are to be able to build up the church," said a program manager at a medical supplies company who talked about the skills he gained when he was in the military.[18]

Others viewed the impact of their work on the church as more financial. Donating to their congregation, with money they make through their paid employment, can be seen as a calling. "We tithe, and so anything I do at work in turn helps my church or any other organizations we wish to give to," explained a man who works as a quality control engineer, "so I guess indirectly that's somewhat of a calling."[19]

Extrinsic/within the workplace: Work as a means of serving at work. For those with an extrinsic/within orientation toward their work as a calling, the meaning of work is focused less on the specific tasks or outcomes of the work they do, but the workplace is still seen as a location for serving others. In this case, a sense of calling is experienced when serving those they interact with at work, such as coworkers, customers, clients, venders, students, and so on. The primary sense of serving these others is not through the work itself but through the relationships they develop with others in the workplace. The church has focused much of its attention over the past century on helping people see the ways they can experience calling in this way, focusing less on the work itself and more on the interpersonal engagement that people

---

[18]F@W_ST09, Black man, age 50, program manager, evangelical, interview conducted November 2, 2018.
[19]F@W_ST75, White man, age 69, reliability and quality engineer, evangelical, interview conducted May 30, 2019.

can have at work. Encouraging people to be moral exemplars, to share their faith with coworkers, or to extend kindness to colleagues are all consistent with an extrinsic/within approach to calling. Those who talked about their work as a calling in this way most commonly described improving the workplace by supporting others interpersonally, creating a positive workplace culture, or sharing faith values with others in the workplace. They often see work as a place to intentionally practice their faith by being a role model for others.

A man who works as the CFO for a credit union shared with us how he feels called to create a good work environment for his employees, saying, "As a manager I try to be a good moral example, and it's more than just the religious background, but you want to make it an ethical place to work, treat people fairly, support them in their career, whatever direction they're going, or however they're growing or learning, support them."[20] While his position as a CFO allows him to work toward this goal, the nature of his specific workplace, a credit union, is not essential toward achieving this end.

Several teachers we spoke with also saw themselves as role models, including a woman who teaches Spanish.[21] "Yes, 100 percent," she said, when asked if she sees her work as a calling. "So, definitely I see my job as more than just teaching Spanish. Yeah, ultimately, I want them to walk out of my classroom knowing Spanish. That's a huge goal, but I also want them to walk out of my classroom having had a glimpse of true Christian love from me and from their classmates, and a good example of what living a life with Jesus is like." A music teacher told us his students often have "emotional baggage" and that he tries to help them through these challenges: "I think that is more my calling than 'I'm gonna make this kid really good on the clarinet.' And that's

---

[20]F@W_ST10, White man, age 59, CFO for credit union, evangelical, interview conducted November 6, 2018.

[21]F@W_ST21, White woman, age 25, Spanish teacher, evangelical, interview conducted December 3, 2018.

important, too, and serves its own purpose, but I definitely feel more called to the nonmusical parts of the music education."[22]

Other workers described feeling that work gives them an opportunity to express their faith values in social situations and that this provides a sense of meaning during everyday workplace activities. For example, a man who works as a criminal investigator told us, "I believe that I'm called not only to stand up for the rights of those who have been harmed and those who have been wronged but also to really make sure that I exude some very Judeo-Christian values to people who might not otherwise experience them."[23] While it seems he finds some intrinsic meaning in his work helping others, his sense of calling also comes from sharing his faith-informed values with those he comes into contact with through his work. This sort of sentiment came up often.

There is a sense here that these workers have some intention to foster religious beliefs or morals in others like their own. Some we interviewed were more explicit about this. While the majority of workers we interviewed do not think work is an appropriate place for unsolicited discussions of their faith, several we spoke with do see the workplace as a site for evangelizing. Overlapping with the idea of being a role model, a mainline Protestant maintenance manager who often hires formerly incarcerated individuals told us how he felt he fulfilled a calling at work by sharing his values with one of his employees and contributing to his conversion: "One inmate that I had was a Muslim when I hired him, and when he got out, he was a Christian. I want to say I had a little bit of help during that 'cause I was going through a rough time at work myself, and he saw me never really lose my cool, lose my temper, I kept on plugging away doing my job, and maybe he said, 'Hey, you know, I want to be like him.'"[24]

---

[22] F@W_ST78, White man, age 28, music teacher, Catholic, interview conducted June 3, 2019.

[23] F@W_ST49, Black man, age 38, criminal investigator, evangelical, interview conducted February 6, 2019.

[24] F@W_ST70, White man, age 54, maintenance, mainline, interview conducted May 22, 2019.

PRACTICAL WAYS FOR CHRISTIANS TO ENGAGE WORK AS A CALLING

Our discussion to this point has described the ways that individuals we interviewed thought about their work as a calling. The various approaches they take may be helpful to us as we think about how our faith *should* influence our view of work. Are there ways we can learn from the Reformers, the Puritans, and Christians of today to consider how God might want us to conceive of and approach our daily tasks of work? In the remainder of this chapter, we address some of the ways that Christians might use our research to think about their work and the ways it can contribute to a broad Christian mission.

A number of years ago, sociologist David Graeber wrote a magazine article called, "On the Phenomenon of Bullshit Jobs," in which he posited that roughly half of the jobs in our modern world are meaningless make-work jobs.[25] The article struck a nerve and had over a million hits. It was subsequently translated into twelve languages, and Graeber went on to write a book on the topic, with testimonials from people around the world who found their work pointless.[26] Clearly, those with whom the argument resonated did not see their work as important to God or neighbor. But just as clearly, make-work jobs are not what God intended.

From the opening chapters of Genesis, we see the importance and intrinsic value of both humans and work. At creation, God is portrayed as a worker who makes good things. Human beings are created in God's image (Genesis 1:27), and therefore designed and mandated by God to work—not simply to fill the time but also, as expressed in the creation mandate, to partner with God in extending and continuing the work of creation that God began.[27] To accomplish this ongoing work, we see

---

[25]David Graeber, "On the Phenomenon of Bullshit Jobs: A Work Rant," *Strike Magazine* 3 (2013), https://strikemag.org/bullshit-jobs/.

[26]David Graeber, *Bullshit Jobs* (New York: Simon & Schuster, 2018).

[27]Genesis 1:28 is often referenced as the creation mandate. "God blessed them and said to them, 'Be fruitful and increase in number; fill the earth and subdue it. Rule over the fish in the sea and the birds in the sky and over every living creature that moves on the ground.'"

God endow humans with creativity and provide them with relationships to God and one another. He gives Adam and Eve the ability to
make choices. God also models rest from work. These are high and lofty
gifts and expectations; but, of course, before we get too far into the
story, we see sin enter the world when Adam and Eve disobey God's
command not to eat from the tree of the knowledge of good and evil.
The consequence is that toil, thorns, and thistles are introduced to the
fields where Adam works. What God designed at creation becomes
cursed in the fall, and this affects every aspect of our lives and our
world, including our experience of work.

Most of us have had experiences of work that are less than ideal in
one way or another. Elaine remembers a summer job she had as a college
student in the library of her university where for several hours a day she
erased pencil marks in books. The work was boring; it was hard not to
fall asleep and—even though there were no smartphones then—she was
incredibly distracted. What is more, the books were about entomology
(the study of bugs) and, to her, not even that interesting to read. As the
summer wore on, she got slower and slower at her job because she dis-
liked it so much. She was tempted to show up to work late and leave
early. While the other students who worked alongside her managed to
continue their work, she finally got so slow and so distracted that she
was fired! This was only a summer job, and her performance did not
end up having a big impact on her life outcomes, but it did highlight for
her the challenges that particularly boring work can create. Think about
doing this kind of job for months or years on end.

But it is not just boring work that can become tedious or toilsome.
Many of us have had experiences at work that reflect aspects of the fall.
Perhaps we have had difficult relationships with coworkers, the stress of
overwork, or disconnects between our intentions and the outcomes of
our work (maybe reflective of the thorns and thistles that God told Adam
would arise even though they had not been planned or planted). Many of
us have also experienced the consequences of baggage that we and others

bring to work—such as bullying, office politics, unethical behaviors, and problems in our personal lives that spill over into the workplace.

Of course, the story does not end in Genesis. The rest of the Bible points toward the redemption that God provides through Jesus' death and resurrection. This redemptive act is one that overcomes death, furthers the work of creation, pushes back against the effects of the fall, and at a very personal level redeems us to be in relationship with God, both here on the earth and into eternity. As redeemed people, there are implications for our work. Titus 2:14 says, "[Jesus] gave himself for us to redeem us from all wickedness and to purify for himself a people that are his very own, eager to do what is good." How can we do what is good at work? Can our work become redemptive?

FINDING THE INTRINSIC VALUE IN WORK

One of the ways we can engage God's purposes in our work is to recognize the ways that the work we do is meaningful. We have three suggestions: (1) recognize how our work furthers the work of creation, (2) identify ways our work mitigates the effects of the fall, and (3) reframe toilsome aspects of work.

Furthering the work of creation. First, we should examine our work for ways in which it is or can become more consistent with God's purposes at creation. As we already discussed, in the beginning God made humans in the image of God, gave each person gifts and talents that reflect God's own character, placed humans in community, designed them to have creativity, and gave them the ability to make choices. God called humans to co-labor in continuing the work of creation and also gave them the gift of sabbath rest. So, as we consider the work we do, we should examine how it can contribute to God's intent for people and work as designed at creation. Are there aspects of our work that tap into the particular gifts and talents that God has given us? Does our work exercise our creativity? Give us opportunity for decision making and autonomy? Cultivate community or allow us to be in relationship with others? Are we working in an organization that creates things or serves others in a meaningful way? Do we have the opportunity to make, distribute, or sell useful or beautiful things? Does our work engage in a healthy rhythm of work and rest? Does our work give us opportunity to care for God's creation in a large or small way? All of these questions can be asked to examine ways that our work might be carrying forward the purposes God embedded in creation.

We spoke with several individuals who define their work as a continuation of the work of creation. "I try very hard to be a good steward of everything that I'm entrusted with, whether the soil that we take care of, or the finances that we're given, the children—every part of it," said a farmer in Oklahoma, talking about the ways he sees his daily work as redemptive and reflective of God's intent for humans and work embedded in creation.[28] "Even something as simple as the equipment, to try to take care of it as best as we can. . . . We try to be very, very honest. We plant a crop, intending to harvest the crop, not intending to collect an insurance payment."

A graphic artist described the ways he sees his work contributing to God's purposes through the creation of beauty.[29] He believes that God has gifted him with the ability "to add beauty to the world and inspire people. I think that's very godly as well," he said. "It's uplifting, it helps people feel better, it helps them expand their thinking, their horizons. . . . I think beautiful art is—I think art is a great thing in the world."

These are just two small examples of work that is seen as meaningful because it accomplishes God's purposes established at creation. Any work that enhances human dignity, gives people autonomy, exercises creativity, results in useful and needed goods and services, contributes to healthy relationships, or provides healthy rhythms of work and rest can be redemptive work.

---

[28]F@W_ST87, White man, age 35, farmer, evangelical, interview conducted June 14, 2019.
[29]F@W_ST43, Black man, age 48, graphic artist, evangelical, interview conducted January 29, 2019.

Mitigating the effects of the fall. A second way to recognize how our work can be redemptive is to look for ways it might push back against the effects of the fall. For example, with the fall, injustice, sickness, and death entered the world, so jobs that work toward justice or provide healing are redemptive because they are mitigating the effects of the fall. Those who are in legal or medical professions might fairly easily be able to understand their work in this way. But justice and healing can be found in many kinds of jobs. "I get exposed to a lot of different kinds of people . . . [who are] seeking that redemption," said a young real-estate project manager who described how her job allows her to serve people from difficult backgrounds who are seeking to turn their lives around.[30] Her faith, she said, "helps me relate better to the people that I serve at my work because . . . my ultimate goal is to build affordable housing, to house people who are in need." She is using her work to address the brokenness that has resulted in a lack of housing.

Since the fall also resulted in broken relationships, any work that seeks to solve conflict or restore relationships is redemptive work. Those who work as therapists or mediators readily fit this category, but it can also apply to anyone who works to resolve conflict in their relationships at work. A state district representative who serves his local community told us, "In this current political climate, you have a lot of angry people out there who will call in and say some pretty unkind things. . . . I know it's cliché to say, but you know, what would Jesus do? You know he wouldn't lash back . . . and so that's one thing that I think has helped me in this job is really how I converse with some of the angrier people."[31] In this way, he is doing redemptive work by trying to create paths toward reconciliation with those he encounters in his job.

---

[30]F@W_ST180, Asian woman, age 31, real estate project manager, Catholic, interview conducted December 16, 2019.

[31]F@W_ST13, Asian man, age 32, political representative, evangelical, interview conducted November 15, 2018.

Transforming toil. In some jobs, it might be difficult to find examples of how the work is contributing to the activity of creation or mitigating the effects of the fall. We might find ourselves in positions without power and where the culture does not support creativity, beauty, or the intrinsic value of others. We might not see how the goods we produce or the services we provide are making things better for others. We may not feel that our work is contributing toward making things right in our fallen world. Even in these jobs, however, it is possible to find ways that God's redemptive activity is at play. We believe there is another way of identifying the intrinsic value of our work through reframing the work that we are doing. This reframing can involve either reconceptualizing the importance of the work itself or a new understanding of the ways that our work may be shaping our own souls.

Years ago, Denise was at the hospital in labor with her fourth child. The baby was being induced, so she spent the early part of the day waiting for labor to kick in. Consequently, she had the opportunity for long conversations with her nurse, Catherine. She was a wonderful Christian woman who loved her job and did it well. At one point, Catherine was talking about a friend who was training to be a dental hygienist. "Can you imagine a worse job?" she asked. "Putting your hands in people's mouths all day?!" Denise laughed out loud because Catherine had just completed checking her dilation; and if there is anything grosser than putting your hands in people's mouths all day, it might be the work of a labor-and-delivery nurse who is dealing with all manner of bodily fluids in the course of a shift. When Denise expressed this thought, Catherine was genuinely surprised. "But I have a great job!" she said. "I get to welcome babies into the world!" And of course, she was right. But all jobs have elements of toil. It is what we focus on as we do the work that can sometimes determine whether we experience a job as meaningful or toilsome. Cognitive reappraisal can help us think through what could be meaningful about any particular job. We would hope that Catherine's dental hygienist friend understood her work as helping people maintain healthy smiles.

Bill Pollard, past CEO of ServiceMaster, tells a story about a time the company won a contract at a failing hospital.[32] The ServiceMaster team was training the existing hospital custodial staff on the ServiceMaster products and systems. They explained to the staff that the work was not primarily about cleaning floors and toilets; rather, their work was to partner with the medical staff in ensuring that patients could get well by reducing their germ exposure. When the job was reframed in this way, the attitudes and behaviors of those doing the custodial work changed. The toil the workers experienced had been reduced. Perhaps not surprising, their performance improved too.

FINDING THE EXTRINSIC VALUE OF WORK

While it is important for us to identify particular ways that our specific work can contribute to God's redemptive work on earth, the experience of working, no matter what the work entails, should also be understood as part of our calling. "I'm prepared to contend that the primary location for spiritual formation is the workplace," wrote the late pastor and scholar Eugene Peterson.[33] It only makes sense that the place where we spend the single largest percentage of our waking hours would be what God uses to shape our lives and character. In an effort to find intrinsic value in our work, we may inadvertently minimize the extrinsic value of work—how it provides a pathway to important ends outside the work itself. These ends include the ways we show up, the values we demonstrate, and how we view others at work. Perhaps to the most important end, God can use our work to shape our own character and soul.

Values: Hard work and integrity. Over and over again in our interviews, people told us that their faith motivated them to work hard at

---

[32]See William C. Pollard, *The Soul of the Firm* (Grand Rapids, MI: Zondervan, 1996).
[33]Eugene H. Peterson, *Christ Plays in Ten Thousand Places: A Conversation in Spiritual Theology* (Grand Rapids, MI: Eerdmans, 2005), 127.

whatever it was they were doing. Some quoted the verse from the beginning of this chapter, "Whatever you do, work at it with all your
heart, as working for the Lord" (Colossians 3:23). Working hard and
acting with integrity at work were frequently mentioned as ways
people could be mindful of the sacred in their work. Many Christians
made it plain that they thought about *how* they did their work because
they believed that the effort and quality they put in was a way they
served God. A maintenance technician told us, for example, that he
refused to cut corners in his work, even when doing so would be
cheaper and faster.[34] "I'm committed to do the best job I possibly can,"
he said. "And the reasoning for that is my faith, not just good reputation or good standing."

A sixty-five-year-old delivery driver was even more clear about his
reasons for working hard at his job.[35] "The Bible talks about me being
an ambassador or representative of God. And so, the way I work, the
kind of person I present myself as, not only reflects on me but reflects
on the God that I put my trust in. . . . I want to bear the family resem-
blance and be like him, and properly represent him, so I do my work
well," he explained.

Across all kinds of work and levels of organizations, from laborers to
professionals, we heard similar themes: "I am doing God's work here . . .
to honor him and to glorify him" (manager); "I have a very strong work
ethic. . . . Everything I do is done unto God" (administrative assistant);
"I try not to think of it as I'm doing it for a client. I'm doing it for God"
(artist).[36] The outcome of the work itself was not the focus for these
workers but rather the way in which the work was accomplished.

---

[34]F@W_ST44, White man, age 31, maintenance technician, evangelical, interview conducted January 30, 2019.

[35]F@W_ST100, White/Hispanic man, age 65, delivery driver, evangelical, interview conducted July 15, 2019.

[36]F@W_ST15, White woman, age 47, manager of community engagement, evangelical, interview conducted November 20, 2018; F@W_ST34, White woman, age 32, administrative assistant, evangelical, interview conducted January 8, 2019; F@W_ST43, Black man, age 48, graphic artist, evangelical, interview conducted January 29, 2019.

Recognizing others as image bearers. Another way our work can shape our character is through how we see and relate to others, whether our coworkers, customers, boss, or someone else with whom we interact because we are working. The idea that God created humans "in the image of God" (Genesis 1:27) has shaped the way both the Christian and Jewish traditions have understood the importance and value of every human being, regardless of their skills, talents, behaviors, attitudes, and ambitions. This idea also seemed to shape the way many of those we spoke with talked about their relationships at work. While it was unusual for us to hear explicitly theological language, we did hear the underlying concepts fairly often. Workers explained that their Christian beliefs influenced the ways they saw others and interacted with them at work.

The importance of acknowledging the dignity of the person came through quite strongly from workers in the medical field, perhaps because medical work focuses so uniquely on individual patients. One nurse explained that she works sixteen-hour shifts and that it is easy to dehumanize patients when you are tired or overwhelmed by patient loads.[37] But she went on to say, "I think that my faith gives me the ability to show each patient the love of God and to keep a smile on my face, to keep being there for them and their needs." Similarly, a paramedic told us that his faith "gives me more patience with my fellow human beings [because] we're all children on God's earth and we need to respect each other."[38] This emphasis on the importance of the person extended beyond patients to others at work. A physician, for example, told us that her faith motivates her to "treat people kindly and decently, and you treat everybody that way, from the people that are picking up the trash to the CEO."[39]

---

[37] F@W_ST86, White woman, age 21, nurse, evangelical, interview conducted June 13, 2019.
[38] F@W_ST110, White man, age 78, paramedic, mainline, interview conducted August 6, 2019.
[39] F@W_ST137, Black woman, age 43, physician, evangelical, interview conducted September 23, 2019.

Several individuals we spoke with discussed how their view of the importance of others influenced their willingness to show patience in the moment and acted as a reminder to bring their frustrations to God. A grocery store clerk explained that some of her coworkers "don't wanna do much," and "you have to be patient with [them]," she said, describing how her Christian views shape her interactions with others.[40] "And when customers are rude to you, you just gotta think, you know, maybe they're havin' a bad day. And you pray, 'God, give 'em a better day.'" Similarly, several workers told us how their faith led them to apologize to others at work. A manager who works in retail told us that there had been situations in which he had not viewed his employees the way that he should and treated them unkindly.[41] When that happens, his faith reminds him to act differently because others are made in God's image. "I go back to that point and talk to the person and say look, what I did was inappropriate or, you know, not the right way to handle myself, and . . . I want to apologize to you," he said.

A public prosecutor said that sometimes it is hard to think highly of people he encounters in his work but told us:

> I always try to see the redeemable qualities in the people I'm going after, the people I'm prosecuting. I always try to keep in mind that [sighs]—that everyone who goes through the system, . . . they're someone's child. They might be someone's sibling. They might be someone's parent. And in all those relationships, they're someone's friend. In all those relationships, there's something that the person they're in relation to finds redeeming about them. And so, I try to keep that in mind.[42]

Other workers similarly told us about struggles they had viewing certain others in their workplace as made in God's image. For example, another man who works with those in the prison system told us,

[40]F@W_ST132, White woman, age 58, grocery store clerk, evangelical, interview conducted September 12, 2019.

[41]F@W_ST183, White man, age 54, retail management, evangelical, interview conducted December 17, 2019.

[42]F@W_ST136, Hispanic man, age 39, lawyer, mainline, interview conducted September 19, 2019.

I was guilty of dehumanizing the individuals that we were serving, because even though they are incarcerated, they are still people. . . . I felt myself falling victim to the sense that these people did something that put 'em in prison, so they aren't a person. So, over some deep reflection, I had to make a change in my attitude. . . . I'm not a person to pass judgement on them, that's not my place in this world; that's the Lord's job. . . . My faith played a very large role in that.[43]

Fundamentally, the belief that someone else is created by God can determine the way we interact with them, shaping us as well as them in that interaction.

Toil shapes our soul. Earlier in this chapter, we discussed ways that toilsome work—work that is difficult or dirty—might be reframed to become more meaningful if we could identify the ways in which it was serving others or contributing to the world in some positive way. But sometimes toil cannot be reframed in this way. No amount of cognitive reappraisal can diminish the toil experienced in some aspects of work. In this circumstance, we may want to consider how toil might provide an opportunity for personal or spiritual growth or the capacity we might have to change what counts as toil. That is, rather than focus on what is wrong with a situation, focus on how it is changing you or giving you the chance to extend forgiveness, grace, or trust. Significant adversity at work creates a shakeup of our expectations of others and ourselves. It provides us with an opportunity to reassess what is important—what we will keep and what we will jettison—and to develop new skills and confidence, or perhaps greater acceptance of ourselves and others. It can help us to be more gracious and less demanding.

In his research on corporate leaders, organizational psychologist Paul Yost found that one of the most common ways people tend to learn on the job is through some type of difficulty, perhaps because of

---

[43]F@W_ST25, Hispanic man, age 36, asset management, Catholic, interview conducted December 7, 2018.

the strong emotional impact such experiences can trigger.[44] Yost's research asked executives about what had most contributed to their development as a leader. Shepherding others through a personal crisis or having to confront someone with a performance problem were commonly referenced as learning experiences. Leading without authority—that is, getting things done through other people without having any direct authority over them—or experiencing leadership setbacks were frequently cited as critical incidents that led to leadership development. Experiencing failure and making mistakes were also identified as opportunities for learning and growth. In other words, professional development for leaders (and probably for nonleaders too) usually does not happen without hardship or toil. So, toil, while unpleasant and difficult to go through, can ultimately lead to a redemptive experience of resiliency and thriving at work. The apostle Paul seems to acknowledge this when he writes, "We also glory in our sufferings, because we know that suffering produces perseverance; perseverance, character; and character, hope" (Romans 5:3-4).

Many people reflect on the most difficult times in their lives as experiences that draw them close to God. In the New Testament Paul reflects on his own experience of suffering from his "thorn in the flesh." The message he received from God was, "My grace is sufficient for you, for my power is made perfect in weakness" (2 Corinthians 12:9). There seems to be something about our most difficult experiences that are used by God to shape us into the kind of people God intends us to be.

REFLECTION QUESTIONS

For everyone

- What are you doing to learn what your particular gifts are? Whom do you need to connect with, or what do you need to read, or

---

[44]P. R. Yost, "Resilience Practices," *Industrial and Organizational Psychology: Perspectives on Science and Practice* 9 (2016): 475-79.

where do you need to go to imagine how God might use your particular gifts in the workplace?

- If we agree that feeling called to one's work is a good thing, how can workplace leaders make space in their organization for workers to experience calling?

- What changes might need to be made to your workplace to make it more just and equitable?

- How can you understand and communicate the value your organization or workplace provides to others?

For faith communities

- To what extent do you think all workers have the power to use their work in service to God and others? To what extent is this message being communicated through your church?

- Are there ways your church could expand discussions about calling to include the self, others, and contexts that are both close to and far from the workplace itself?

4

PROTECTING OURSELVES

Behold, I am sending you out as sheep in the midst of
wolves, so be wise as serpents and innocent as doves.
Beware of men, for they will deliver you over to courts
and flog you . . . and you will be dragged before governors
and kings for my sake, to bear witness before them and
the Gentiles. . . . You will be hated by all for my name's
sake. But the one who endures to the end will be saved.

MATTHEW 10:16-18, 22 ESV

"DO NOT PUT THE WORD of God on the floor!" the student from Sudan snapped at Elaine as she casually set her Bible underneath her chair. At the time Elaine was an undergraduate attending a Christian student conference. The other student told her he had relatives who had been jailed and killed because of their Christian faith. In coming to the United States, he had waded across a river carrying his belongings above his head, trying to avoid alligators and keep dry his family's one copy of the Bible translated into their native language. "Americans do not know what it's like to be persecuted for practicing your faith," he said. "You take so much for granted." Nearly thirty years later, Elaine still remembers keenly the shame she felt at his words. She wondered, *Am I suffering enough because of my faith? Am I wrong to complain if I experience mild othering at school or at work, so little compared to what Christians experience in other places in the world?*

There are many Christians around the world who are persecuted because of their Christian faith. They have their homes and livelihoods taken away. Some are physically injured or killed. Both of us have been encouraged by our church pastors to pray for the persecuted church. We have also been told repeatedly, through both the Bible and stories of heralded Christian martyrs, that we will face discrimination and even persecution as Christians. When persecution does happen, Christians are told they will receive rewards in heaven *because of* it: "Blessed are those who are persecuted because of righteousness, for theirs is the kingdom of heaven" (Matthew 5:10).

Compared with Christians in other parts of the world, we might wonder whether those of us in the United States are actually suffering *enough* for our faith, whether we are wrong to complain when we experience discrimination or harassment because of our expression of faith at work. Yet, our research finds that Christians do report experiences of religious discrimination and harassment at work. Our studies show that a large number of Christians feel a sense of mistreatment at work due to their faith. We wondered whether expecting persecution might prime American Christians to be more likely to see religious discrimination in circumstances that others would not be as quick to label discrimination. Our interviews helped us to understand better the experiences that lead to perceptions of religious discrimination in the workplace.

In one sense, when we think about persecution, the first thing that comes to mind might be the kinds of experiences that Elaine's friend had had—significant, pervasive, negative, and even life-threatening experiences that are targeted at a person because of their religious beliefs or identity. While it might be possible to come up with extreme examples of religious persecution in the United States, such examples are not at all common or representative for US Christians and certainly are not typical in most American workplaces. Even so, many Christians do feel that they are treated differently—and often worse—at work because of the way others react to their religious identity. But what counts as religious discrimination in the workplace?

The law provides one kind of answer. Title VII of the 1964 Civil Rights Act makes it illegal to discriminate against people at work due to their religion. Most employers are not allowed to consider religion when making decisions about hiring, promoting, compensating, or firing employees (there are some exceptions for those with religious missions, such as churches or church-affiliated organizations). Employers are also required to make reasonable accommodations for people's religious practices at work—things such as time off for religious practices or allowances for religious attire—as long as those accommodations do not cause undue hardship for the employer. Both the Equal Employment Opportunity Commission and court cases have clarified this law in the years since it was passed. Today the courts recognize harassment as a type of discrimination. If someone is criticized for their religious beliefs, or if jokes are regularly made about the practices of a particular religious group, that is construed as discrimination from a legal perspective.

Under certain circumstances Christians do experience faith-based discrimination. Our survey data shows that a large number of Christians say they have experienced mistreatment at work due to their faith or because of the way others react to their religious identity. Many of those we interviewed felt that they had experienced some measure of discrimination. They discussed experiencing comments and behaviors from others at work that made them feel like outsiders in their own workplaces. Sometimes the stories they shared with us would likely meet the legal definition of religious discrimination. Other times the behavior in question would likely *not* meet the legal definition of

religious discrimination—or perhaps would be very hard to prove—
and yet it caused negative repercussions for the person experiencing
the behavior. Some people left their jobs because of the ways they had
been treated. Others withdrew or stopped engaging in the same way in
their workplaces. A number of them simply resolved not to be as overt
about their faith at work.

There are certain workplaces where Christians are more likely to
claim they have experienced discrimination: where Christians are in
the minority, where it is a cultural expectation of the profession that
individuals *not* express a religious identity (e.g., in science and technology occupations), and in regions where there are not as many Christians. We believe it is important for Christians to understand the kinds
of religious discrimination that Christians and other people of faith
experience in the workplace and to consider how we might respond to
it when it does occur, both when it is targeted at us and when it may be
directed toward others.

**Christians who report experiences of religious discrimination
by industry or occupation**

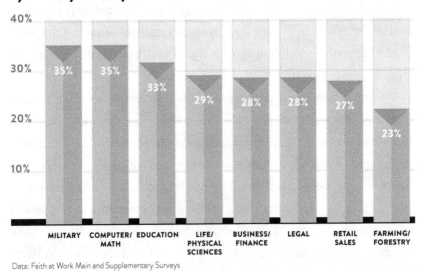

Data: Faith at Work Main and Supplementary Surveys

Figure 4.1

HOW CHRISTIANS EXPERIENCE
DISCRIMINATION IN THE WORKPLACE

When Denise was in graduate school, she heard her professors discuss a job candidate for a faculty position at the university. The candidate had attended a faith-based school, and while he never discussed his faith openly during the interview process, it was clear from his vitae that he was a Christian. The professors raised concerns about the candidate's ability to be an impartial scholar because of his personal faith commitments, and he was ultimately not offered the job. His Christian faith, it appeared, was not welcomed in the academy.

Both of us have since experienced firsthand the kinds of assumptions and stereotypes that can be made about Christians. As we have moved into our respective careers as scholars, interacting in academic circles with colleagues who are not Christians or who have no faith, we have regularly heard negative comments about Christians before others know our own faith identities. We have heard other academics express concerns that research about religion at work that is conducted by scholars who have a personal faith commitment cannot possibly be unbiased, and therefore any research findings in this domain are viewed with suspicion. Alternatively, some have wondered aloud whether research focused on faith-based topics in the workplace has any import or value, since they do not believe religion belongs at work under any condition. When we attend academic conferences, we have learned to be careful how we talk about our own religious identities because doing so can shut down the conversation; people do not know how to respond. They wonder whether, because of our Christian faith, we have political or social viewpoints that are outside the academic norm. They are concerned that we will be judgmental toward others.

As a scholar who is a Christian and studies the sociology of religion, Elaine has experienced some of these challenges in various forms for most of her career, with some arguing that people who are personally religious have less scholarly objectivity than others. Although Denise has worked in Christian higher education for most of her career, she has sometimes experienced this kind of subtle suspicion from those outside her college or university setting. There have been concerns that her institutional affiliation at a Christian university will limit what she can research or talk about in the classroom. More recently, her employment at Wheaton College, a flagship evangelical Christian school, has brought the comment that she is "not like most evangelicals," with the commenter seeming to intend the statement as a positive affirmation. While these kinds of comments and concerns are experienced as "othering," we have typically not felt like we are discriminated against in the workplace because of our faith. But many Christians do feel this way.

In our survey, 37 percent of evangelical Christians, 21 percent of mainline Protestant (Methodist or Episcopalian) workers, and 22 percent of Catholic workers reported experiencing some form of religious discrimination in the workplace. One man described how, during his first job out of college as a landscape architect, "In my emails I would put, you know, a little Christian message underneath, and one of my managers had asked me not to do that, and I thought that was persecution."[1] This feeling was also based on a previous discussion he had with his manager, who was Baha'i, about the distinctions between their faiths. His manager "took it offensively," he said, "when I was able to kind of calmly give him . . . a reason for why I believe what I believe. He didn't like what I had to say."

Christians, especially evangelicals we talked with, said they experience marginalization in how they are unfairly stereotyped by coworkers as judgmental, hypocritical, "having the wrong thinking," or being narrow-minded. To a lesser extent, they link experiences of negative treatment in the workplace to expressions of personal piety (such as listening to Christian music, displaying religious symbols, observing religious holidays, or not drinking alcohol) or moral qualms (such as

---

[1]F@W_ST50, Hispanic man, age 48, co-owner of landscape architect business, evangelical, interview conducted February 6, 2019.

not wanting to break the rules, engage in unethical behavior, or participate in workplace conversations that they see as inappropriate). Some workers use terms such as *holy*—which might seem positive in certain contexts—in pejorative ways against their Christian colleagues. A criminal investigator expresses his faith openly in the workplace.[2] He also uses his faith to draw specific moral boundaries, such as not getting drunk with colleagues or lying at work. One woman told us her coworkers at a past job would make fun of her, saying things like, "Oh, there's the praise lady or the holy roller."[3] A woman working as a nurse told us she felt shamed for her moral concerns when coworkers called her "goody two-shoes" after she challenged them directly for using racist or inappropriate language.[4]

We also heard Christian workers say they were marginalized by nonreligious coworkers and workers of other faiths for displaying religious symbols or taking Christian religious holidays seriously for their religious content. A woman working in finance told us that her supervisor had asked her to take down a Christmas angel decoration on her desk, though nonreligious decorations were deemed acceptable in the office.[5] An art teacher said she was ridiculed by a supervisor for observing Ash Wednesday.[6] Another woman who works as an information systems analyst recalled working a ten-hour shift on Good Friday, then getting a call from her manager upon leaving work in which she was reprimanded.[7] "Why are you not at the office? You have a lot of work. [Your colleague] is complaining that you don't do enough work," she remembered the manager saying in a harsh tone. When she

---

[2] F@W_ST49, Black man, age 38, criminal investigator, evangelical, interview conducted February 6, 2019.

[3] F@W_ST135, Hispanic woman, age 27, packer, evangelical, interview conducted September 17, 2019.

[4] F@W_ST98, White woman, age 60, registered nurse, evangelical, interview conducted July 10, 2019.

[5] F@W_ST38, Hispanic woman, age 51, finance, evangelical, interview conducted January 11, 2019.

[6] F@W_ST42, White woman, age 31, art teacher, Catholic, interview conducted January 24, 2019.

[7] F@W_ST169, Hispanic woman, age 45, information systems analyst, Catholic, interview conducted December 5, 2019.

reminded her manager that it was Good Friday, she was surprised by his response: "Your religion is not going to pay your food or rent or give you a promotion."

WHEN CHRISTIANS ARE IN THE MINORITY

There is not much scholarly research on religious discrimination among Christian workers in the United States, but several studies have found that Christians perceive religious discrimination in specific work contexts where they are particularly underrepresented or where the norms of the occupation are considered by occupational insiders or those in leadership to be different from the norms of Christian faith. "I used to work at a newspaper and they're like, you know, 'Why would you believe all that?'" said a woman who now works as a tutor.[8] It was, in her words, "a very liberal, secular environment."

Where a Christian works can significantly shape whether or how they experience religious discrimination or marginalization. Our research and that of generations of social scientists before us reveals that those who are in the minority—in number and influence—in almost any context are more likely to experience discrimination.[9] We believe this is why our research also shows that Christians who express their religious identity or beliefs at work might experience marginalization or discrimination in one occupation or one regional location but feel supported and encouraged when they express those same beliefs in another job or location. What seems to matter is how similar or different they are from those around them.

The marginalization does not always come from those who do not share the Christian faith. Sometimes it comes from other Christians from different traditions who make up a majority in a particular place.

---

[8] F@W_ST45, White woman, age 48, tutor, evangelical, interview conducted January 30, 2019.
[9] Those who are in the numerical majority but have little power—think about Black South Africans—often experience discrimination and marginalization. But there is something particularly important about both being in the numerical minority and having less power in a situation that creates the conditions for extreme marginalization, othering, and discrimination.

One Christian woman who attends a Presbyterian church in a rural area of the United States described how her former evangelical Christian colleagues at the library where she works had formed negative opinions about her due to her religious affiliation.[10] She explained, "Being Presbyterian, we're kind of known to be a little more [theologically and politically] liberal, and I worked with some people that were very conservative [Christians], and I was viewed as not having the right thinking."

We heard similar experiences of marginalization from those who lived and worked in places where religion played a less prominent role in everyday life. When we asked a man who works at an airport in a major city whether he had ever experienced religious discrimination, he answered "not per se" but said his workplace peers made assumptions about the political beliefs of Christians.[11] They had "their preconceived notions about Christians, and they just refuse to get along," he said, and "if you weren't in their [liberal] club, then you were singled out for destruction." From his conservative perspective, "if you were a person of integrity, you just didn't fit in." Because of an environment that he described as "toxic," he left this job after two years, the shortest work experience of his career.

In our studies over the years, religious individuals who were not evangelical Protestant Christians experienced the Southern United States as disproportionately hostile, and this was largely attributed to the South's evangelical Christian influence. Catholics, as well as atheists and those who are nonreligious, working in the South are more likely to experience workplace religious discrimination, also attributed to the South's evangelical Christian influence, than are individuals from those same groups in the Northeast and the West. But sociologists Christopher Scheitle and Katie Corcoran find that evangelical

---

[10] F@W_ST161, White woman, age 62, sales/office work, mainline, interview conducted November 20, 2019.

[11] F@W_ST80, Black man, age 43, law enforcement, evangelical, interview conducted June 4, 2019.

Protestants living in the West are particularly likely to perceive religious discrimination when compared with evangelical Protestants living in the South. They suggest this may be because Southern Christians "perceive themselves as in less conflict with their surroundings than their counterparts in other regions."[12]

We also find that Christians, especially those who are devout, report greater religious discrimination in some work contexts, such as academia or science. In these work environments, Christians told us they sometimes feel pressure to defend their theological beliefs or provide a rationale for their religious views in ways that feel uncomfortable or invasive.[13] For example, a Christian woman who worked as an assistant professor of English was reticent to describe the challenges she faced in academia as religious discrimination but said the humanities "tend to not always be welcoming towards religious people [and Christians specifically]."[14] She recalled several instances when she was treated differently due to her faith and noted that in a university work environment, "a lot of people will question the validity of your religion, let alone your faith, and dismiss it on those rights." This woman was both a Christian and a Black American and thought she experienced a particular kind of discrimination because of the overlap between her race and faith. These kinds of experiences shaped her desire to pursue other job opportunities, she said, "because this is the kind of place that makes you feel unwelcome."

Sociologist John Schmalzbauer sees religious discrimination against Christians in certain work environments as based in part in the

---

[12]Christopher P. Scheitle and Katie E. Corcoran, "Religious Tradition and Workplace Religious Discrimination: The Moderating Effects of Regional Context," *Social Currents* 5 (2018): 283-300 (see esp. 297).

[13]F@W_ST131, Hispanic man, age 50, marble assembly, Catholic, interview conducted September 11, 2019; F@W_ST49, Black man, age 38, criminal investigator, evangelical, interview conducted February 6, 2019; F@W_ST50, Hispanic man, age 48, co-owner of landscape architect business, evangelical, interview conducted February 6, 2019.

[14]F@W_ST102, Black woman, age 32, assistant professor of English, evangelical, interview conducted July 17, 2019.

tensions some Christians might have with the ways of doing things in an occupation or the type of people whom an occupation generally draws.[15] Elaine and colleagues show in their research that religious academic scientists report discrimination in the workplace more frequently than their nonreligious colleagues do, and Christians in academic science are especially likely to report religious discrimination.[16] This is particularly true for evangelical Christians, who are underrepresented in most sectors of science. Similarly, academic job candidates across many disciplines in higher education are viewed more negatively when they identify as conservative Christian or Mormon.[17]

RACIAL AND RELIGIOUS DISCRIMINATION OVERLAP FOR CHRISTIANS

Feeling othered or discriminated against because of their Christian faith can be another way that people of color disproportionately experience marginalization. Black, Hispanic, and Asian Christians, in particular, told us that they experience discrimination because of their faith in addition to discrimination because of their race or ethnicity, what we call "double marginalization." A Black woman told us she had felt excluded by her coworkers due to her faith.[18] She said she often felt left out of social gatherings and mentioned that "sometimes I've experienced not having close friends in the workplace because I have stood out as a Christian." Importantly, she also told us about experiences of workplace exclusion that she attributed to being the only African American working in her department. While in neither case had she been told why she was being excluded, she made an

---

[15]See John A. Schmalzbauer, *People of Faith: Religious Conviction in American Journalism and Higher Education* (Ithaca, NY: Cornell University Press, 2002).

[16]Scheitle and Corcoran, "Religious Tradition and Workplace Religious Discrimination." See also Elaine Howard Ecklund, *Science vs. Religion: What Scientists Really Think* (New York: Oxford University Press, 2010).

[17]George Yancey, *Compromising Scholarship: Religious and Political Bias in American Higher Education* (Waco, TX: Baylor University Press, 2011).

[18]F@W_ST71, Black woman, age 66, reimbursement analyst, evangelical, interview conducted May 28, 2019.

attribution based on the demographic composition of her workplace. When she was the only racial minority, it seemed more likely that her experiences were due to her race, and when she was a religious minority in a workplace with a lot of other African Americans, she attributed these times of experiencing workplace exclusion to an anti-Christian bias.

Race and religion are often inextricably connected in these situations, making it difficult for Black, Hispanic, and Asian workers to figure out whether the source of their discrimination and feeling othered is due primarily to their race, to their religion, or the overlap between the two. We should note that racial discrimination is more common than religious discrimination for many racial minority groups, but one type of discrimination tends to compound the other. For example, based on our research, over one-quarter of Black workers say they experience religious discrimination, while 77 percent experience racial discrimination.

Some researchers have questioned whether Christians in the United States can experience workplace discrimination due to their faith, since they belong to *the* majority religion in the country. Our research suggests that they can. However, Christians in the United States who do report religious discrimination and harassment at work are most likely to have experiences of marginalization or othering rather than direct and overt persecution due to their faith. These experiences are more common in some contexts and regions than others. While such experiences are real and have negative repercussions for those who are targeted in this way, we wonder whether Christians may be more attentive to them because they are expecting discrimination due to their faith. In the next chapter we explore how those from minority religions in the United States experience religious discrimination at work and how Christians should respond in these situations.

REFLECTION QUESTIONS

For everyone

- What do you think counts as religious discrimination in the workplace?

- What should Christians do when they find themselves being marginalized at work and believe it is because of their faith? Are you more likely to address a comment directly (e.g., "It makes me uncomfortable when you talk about Christians that way because I am one, and it feels demeaning") or to ignore it? What are various ways to engage others about marginalizing religious faith?

- When is it better to address faith-based marginalization informally and interpersonally, and when is it important to pursue organizational remedies or escalation to a supervisor and beyond?

- How attuned are you to the experiences of people of faith who may be different from you? If you are part of the majority religious culture in your workplace, are there ways you may be marginalizing others who are in the minority? How would you know?

- If you are part of the minority religious culture in your workplace, to what extent are you developing relationships with others who have a different set of beliefs but who are also part of the religious minority? What do those relationships look like?

For faith communities

- In what ways does your church talk about experiences of religious discrimination in the workplace?

- Do you feel like your church does a good job of addressing religious discrimination? If so, in what ways? If not, what do you think your church and *the* church should do differently?

- Does your church link religious discrimination to other kinds of discrimination (such as racial or gender discrimination?) How does your church do this? Is it effective?

5

PROTECTING OTHERS

*So in everything, do to others what you would have them
do to you, for this sums up the Law and the Prophets.*

MATTHEW 7:12

MARTHA EXPERIENCES RELIGIOUS discrimination.[1] She works
as a salesperson in Louisiana for a company that sells industrial ma-
chinery, and she is a convert to Islam. Martha told us that after she
converted, her colleagues relentlessly bullied her. For example, one day
a coworker wore a shirt with "a machine gun on it and 'Infidel' on it,"
she said. "That was a play to intimidate me because it was—I was very
new to Islam, very excited about what I was learning, and it was ritual
ridicule." After someone put up signs in the office attacking her new-
found faith, she called in management, but they did nothing to help her.
They actually harassed her more, she said. "One of them said something
about, 'I tried to see your point of view, but your point of view is stupid,'
and another person said, 'It must be great coming to work and not
having to do anything [a reference to Martha taking time to pray],'" she
recalled. "Just ugly stuff, really, really ugly stuff."

---

[1] F@W_ST111, White woman, age 63, retired, Muslim, interview conducted August 7, 2019.

It is tempting for Christians to shift into a defensive posture and to seek to protect ourselves against unfair assumptions, stereotypes, and personal slights. Evangelical Christians in particular report experiencing more workplace conflicts due to religion compared with those from other Christian traditions or those who are nominal Christians. We definitely do not want to minimize the reality of these experiences. But here is where we also want to introduce a new way. We think that faithfulness in our current moment may require less attention to ourselves as Christians and more attention to others. In particular, faithfulness may require paying more attention to those from religious minorities in the United States (especially Muslims and Jews), who are *more* likely than Christians to be experiencing workplace conflict due to their religious identity.

CHRISTIANS HAVE A RESPONSIBILITY TO PROTECT THE "OTHER"

As we have seen, Christians in the United States do perceive religious discrimination in the workplace. But our research over the past two decades shows clearly that *it is not primarily Christians who experience the most consequential workplace discrimination*. So then, how should Christians in the workplace respond when those from other faiths and those of no faith are experiencing discrimination due to their beliefs? Based on the many examples of biblical teachings that emphasize Jesus' heart for the poor and the marginalized, we argue that Christians, especially those in positions of power and leadership (which is many of us!), have a specific faith-based responsibility to fight for those who are othered, which in the majority of workplaces is *not* Christians. We need to fight for others in no small part as an acknowledgment that all—even those whose faith perspectives we might not agree with—are made in the image of God. To do this we need to understand the groups that are the most marginalized in our workplaces and the kinds of discrimination they face.

We want to say up front that those in leadership roles may need to pay particularly close attention to how those from different religious traditions might experience the workplace, and then work hard to address religious discrimination as well as foster the kinds of positive conditions that make religious discrimination less likely to occur.

When we look at the data we have collected on experiences of workplace discrimination, we find that more than 60 percent of Muslim workers and more than 50 percent of Jewish workers perceive religion-related discrimination at work. This varies by region, however, with the Western and Southern United States representing the regions of the country where the largest share of Muslim workers (84 percent and 72 percent, respectively) experience discrimination, and the Midwest representing the region of the country where the largest share of Jewish workers (62 percent) experience discrimination. Overall, among the religious groups we surveyed, Muslims report by far the most discrimination in the workplace. About 17 percent of Muslims said they experienced religious discrimination often or very often. By comparison, only 3 percent of evangelical Christians reported experiencing religious discrimination often or very often.[2]

Jewish and Muslim workers are also most likely to experience other forms of discrimination at work. Among the workers we surveyed, 60 percent of Muslim workers and 44 percent of Jewish workers who reported religious discrimination also reported at least one other form of discrimination, highlighting the degree to which other aspects of identity might be linked to experiences of religious discrimination for some groups. This is especially the case for women—33 percent of women who have experienced religious discrimination have also experienced gender discrimination, compared with only 8 percent of men.

---

[2]Interestingly, a higher proportion of those who identify as "other Christian" reported having ever experienced religious discrimination (55 percent). This includes Mormons and others who may not identify with mainline and evangelical traditions. Their experiences seem to depart from evangelical and mainline Christians in notable ways. Only 2 percent of mainline Protestants and 2 percent of Catholics reported experiencing religious discrimination often or very often.

Jewish and Muslim respondents who report experiences of religious discrimination by region of the United States

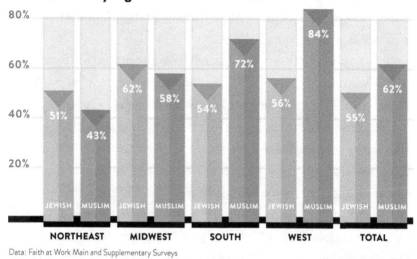

Data: Faith at Work Main and Supplementary Surveys

Figure 5.1

Workers who claim a sexual-minority orientation are also more likely than other groups to experience religious discrimination. Among that group, 53 percent of those who identify as sexual minorities also report having experienced workplace religious discrimination, and our interviews show that those who are sexual minorities often perceive being discriminated against in the workplace by Christians.

One-third of workers without a religious tradition say they have experienced discrimination for having no religion—almost the same percentage as that of evangelicals who have experienced religious discrimination and more than Catholics. Those who are not religious—including atheists, agnostics, and those who simply do not identify with a religious tradition—are a growing population in the United States. Like the example of Joann that we shared at the beginning of this book, these people told us about being denied work opportunities because of their lack of religion, said that others would make negative assumptions about their morals and ethics because they did not have a religious faith, spoke of how they experienced a general sense of social isolation in organizations where the management or leadership is overtly Christian, and said that they were sometimes conflicted about how to respond when others assumed that they were religious, and specifically assumed that they were Christian.

"I do notice a lot of religious people have a very hard time accepting people who don't follow their faith. I had an experience, even with my sister, who, when I told her that I didn't want to go to church anymore, her response was, 'You're going to burn in hell,'" said a Black woman who works as an engineer and considers herself agnostic.[3] In the workplace, she said that most people assume those who are Black are also Christian and, "if I mention directly, like, 'Yes, I'm not religious,' then, I might—I will be looked at differently or interacted with differently as well." She said she knows "there are people who would do crazy things, like vandalize a car or they'd leave rude notes," she said, adding, "I don't think it would happen with the people I work with. But it's still the scenario—and I guess this is the downside to not really showing what your faith is. You can't distinguish between casual religious followers and extremist religious followers. And that can have dangers to it as well."

Workplace leaders rarely openly discuss religious discrimination, how it relates to other kinds of discrimination, or what can be done to rectify it or, *better yet*, prevent it in the first place. Organizational scholar of diversity Diether Gebert and colleagues argue that religious expression is the "neglected dimension of diversity" in workplaces.[4] In fact, it was not uncommon for the workers we talked with to not even know that religious discrimination—including treating people differently due to religion—is illegal for most types of workplaces. Religious discrimination appears to be on the rise. Between 1997 (which was the

---

[3]See F@W_ST205, Black woman, age 25, engineer, agnostic, interview conducted May 25, 2021.
[4]See D. Gebert, S. Boerner, E. Kearney, J. E. King Jr., K. Zhang, and L. J. Song, "Expressing Religious Identities in the Workplace: Analyzing a Neglected Diversity Dimension," *Human Relations* 67 (2014): 543-63 (see esp. 543).

first year that the Equal Employment Opportunity Commission began to collect data on religiously based workplace discrimination), and 2023, reports of discrimination based on religion increased by over 250 percent, from 1,709 to 4,341 cases. This growth is much larger than the changes in other forms of discrimination, such as that based on sex or national origin. According to our own survey of working Americans, about 30 percent of US workers reported experiencing religious discrimination at some point in their working lives.

DISCRIMINATION FOR RELIGIOUS MINORITIES

Several of the Jewish and Muslim workers we talked with for our research shared that they had often heard colleagues or clients making antisemitic or Islamophobic remarks and that they regularly encounter religious and cultural stereotypes in the workplace.[5] A number of them talked about intentionally concealing or downplaying their faith in the workplace due to fears about a hostile work environment or because they were trying to mitigate the possibility of religious discrimination. A Muslim gas station owner said she doesn't consider her workplace a safe environment to express her faith, even though she actually owns her business![6] "There are some people who are so hard on me [for being Muslim] that they will not even think about it, and if you even try to explain to them, they won't listen," she said of her customers. "They have their own mindset, [which is all so] negative."

Although less than 2 percent of the US population identifies as Muslim (a number that is likely a result of underreporting given the fear US Muslims have of being mistreated), Muslims represent 28 percent of all complaints of religion-related discrimination made to the

---

[5] F@W_ST108, White man, age 52, consulting, Jewish, interview conducted August 2, 2019; F@W_ST115, Asian man, age 53, engineer, Muslim, interview conducted August 13, 2019. See "Spelling of Antisemitism," International Holocaust Remembrance Alliance, www.holocaustremembrance.com/antisemitism/spelling-antisemitism, for debate about the spelling of the term *antisemitism*.
[6] F@W_ST105, South Asian woman, age 53, gas station owner, Muslim, interview conducted July 29, 2019.

Equal Employment Opportunity Commission.[7] Muslims are consistently the group that reports the most overt religious discrimination at all places in the job pathway, and research findings support Muslim self-reports of discrimination in the workplace. For example, audit experiments have shown that Muslims are less likely than other job applicants to receive callbacks for interviews.[8] Discrimination in the hiring of Muslims, especially for high-status occupations, may further be amplified by the sex of the applicant, the wearing of religious identifiers such as the hijab, and how "Arab-sounding" the applicant's name is.[9] That is, Muslim women who wear a head covering and Muslims with traditional Middle Eastern names are less likely to be hired and promoted compared with Muslims who do not have obvious signifiers of their religious identity.

---

[7]Besheer Mohammed, "New Estimates Show U.S. Muslim Population Continues to Grow," Pew Research Center, January 3, 2018, www.pewresearch.org/fact-tank/2018/01/03/new-estimates-show-u-s-muslim-population-continues-to-grow/; "Religion-Based Charges Filed from 10/01/2000 through 9/30/2011 Showing Percentage Filed on the Basis of Religion-Muslim," U.S. Equal Employment Opportunity Commission, www.eeoc.gov/religion-based-charges-filed-10012000-through-9302011-showing-percentage-filed-basis-religion.

[8]See Alessandro Acquisti and Christina M. Fong,. "An Experiment in Hiring Discrimination via Online Social Networks," *Management Science* 66, no. 3 (March 2020): 1005-24; Michael Wallace, Bradley R. E. Wright, and Allen Hyde, "Religious Affiliation and Hiring Discrimination in the American South: A Field Experiment," *Social Currents* 1 (2014): 189-207. Wallace, Wright, and Hyde show that those who identify as Muslims, alongside pagans and atheists, receive the highest levels of discriminatory behaviors from employers located in the American South. See Bradley R. E. Wright, Michael Wallace, John Bailey, and Allen Hyde, "Religious Affiliation and Hiring Discrimination in New England: A Field Experiment," *Research in Social Stratification and Mobility* 34 (2013): 111-26. Wallace, Wright, and Hyde document that Muslim candidates receive only two-thirds the number of responses from employers compared to their counterparts of other religions.

[9]See Sonia Ghumman and Linda A. Jackson, "Between a Cross and a Hard Place: Religious Identifiers and Employability," *Journal of Workplace Rights* 13 (2008): 259-79. Ghumman and Jackson identify sex as a contributing factor in religious discrimination in workplace settings. See also Sonia Ghumman and Linda A. Jackson, "The Downside of Religious Attire: The Muslim Headscarf and Expectations of Obtaining Employment," *Organizational Behavior* 31 (2010): 4-23; Sonia Ghumman and Ann Marie Ryan, "Not Welcome Here: Discrimination Towards Women Who Wear the Muslim Headscarf," *Human Relations* 66 (2013): 671-98; Daniel Widner and Stephen Chicoine, "It's All in the Name: Employment Discrimination Against Arab Americans," *Sociological Forum* 26 (2011): 806-23. Widner and Chicoine find that "Arab-sounding" names can also increase experiences of discriminatory hiring practices for Muslims. And see a previous article from our data here, https://journals.sagepub.com/doi/10.1177/23780231211070920, retrieved December 30, 2024.

Unlike some of the evangelical Christians we spoke with, who were very attuned to the ways in which they might be viewed as an outsider at work due to their religious beliefs, both Jewish and Muslim workers who were the target of harassment in the workplace often downplayed or overlooked othering that would probably be considered discrimination. A South Asian Muslim man who works as an engineer, for example, mentioned hearing people have conversations in which they said things such as, "Muslims are extremists" or "Send 'em back," though he did not consider this to be discrimination or directed at him explicitly.[10] A Jewish man who works as a consultant recalled a time early in his career when he heard a colleague use the phrase "Jew me down" but said he considered it ignorance rather than discrimination.[11] Most consequential, a Jewish former Air Force officer recalled how during Officer Training School his fellow trainees would make "little jokes" about the Holocaust.[12] At the time, he did not recognize it as antisemitism, he told us, until a fellow cadet came to him and said, "They're saying this because you're Jewish. Don't you realize it?"

Targeted discrimination against Jewish and Muslim workers can sometimes be subtle or ambiguous, making it more difficult for workers to recognize. For example, a Jewish woman working in social services recalled being singled out to visit a sick colleague because it was assumed she could prepare chicken soup, while others in her workplace made comments about her being "good at bookkeeping," both assumptions tapping into long-standing tropes about Jewish people.[13] Unlike

[10]F@W_ST115, Asian man, age 53, engineer, Muslim, interview conducted August 13, 2019.

[11]F@W_ST108, White man, age 52, consulting, Jewish, interview conducted August 2, 2019. The term "Jew down" is an antisemitic trope formed during the Middle Ages about Jews being cheap or prone to hoarding money. See Marcy Oster, "What Does 'Jew Down' Mean, and Why Do People Find It Offensive," Jewish Telegraphic Agency, September 25, 2019, www.jta.org /2019/09/25/culture/what-does-jew-down-mean-and-why-do-people-find-it-offensive.

[12]F@W_ST151, White man, age 78, retired civil servant, Jewish, interview conducted October 23, 2019.

[13]F@W_ST112, White woman, age 49, social services, Jewish, interview conducted August 8, 2019.

the pejorative name calling that we found practicing Christians sometimes experience (such as "holy" and "sanctimonious"), Jewish and
Muslim workers tend to cite instances of antisemitic and anti-Islamic
rhetoric and stereotyping (including "joking") that are tied to long-
standing ideologies (stereotypes that Jews are particularly economi-
cally successful, for example) that have justified actual violence against
Jews and Muslims.

Christian workers should be aware that their Jewish and Muslim
coworkers are more likely to say they are afraid to ask for religious
accommodation or to wear visible religious identifiers in the workplace. Sometimes workers of these faiths told us that they had not
experienced overt discrimination but feared that they might. Several
Jewish and Muslim women told us during our interviews with them
that they actively concealed or downplayed their religious identity in
the workplace to preempt discrimination. They described being hesitant to ask for religious accommodations and their discomfort with
wearing religious attire. "They've always told me, 'You're free to
practice your religion.' . . . But because I don't see other people doing
it, I don't feel comfortable," said a Jewish project manager at an engineering firm, even though she knew there were policies in place to
protect employees from religious discrimination.[14] "And the times that
I did have to pray," she said, "I actually walked outside into a closed
corner in the hallway to do it." She said that as a married woman, she
covered her hair—usually with a wig—in accordance with Orthodox
Jewish practices but then "decided to go in one day [*laughs*] with a
head scarf, and I didn't feel comfortable doing it. But I was just so hot
and so tired of wearing wigs every day. And, when I walked in, I saw
that they did look at me differently, and I felt really uncomfortable,"
she recalled. "But then, after I wore a scarf, I felt I couldn't just switch
back to a wig. So I kept wearing scarves. But every day, I was conscious

---

[14]F@W_ST153, White woman, age 23, student, Jewish, interview conducted October 29, 2019.

of people looking at me, conscious of people judging me, and I was so uncomfortable."

We want you to slow down your reading for a moment here and take this in: part of being a faithful Christian at work is your *awareness of* and *concern for* those who are not Christians.

As we saw in our previous chapter, a number of evangelical Christian workers describe being made to feel like an outsider at work because of their religious beliefs—and this might be a way for them to begin to relate to the experiences of members of minority religions, who also described feeling like they were an outsider or being treated as such in the workplace. Among workers who belong to minority faiths, a sense of not fitting in at work was widespread. They sometimes felt their colleagues defaulted to excluding them from workplace activities such as holiday celebrations, perhaps out of a desire not to transgress perceived religious boundaries. One Indian American Muslim woman working as an optometry technician, for example, said her colleagues were hesitant to approach her about a gift exchange in the work group during the Christmas holiday and were "kind of walking on eggshells around me."[15] She had to reassure them that they could "definitely do a gift exchange, I'm down for that." While workers might exclude those of different faiths from social activities out of a well-intentioned desire not to offend them, it can make those of minority faiths feel even more singled out and different. "There's been a couple of people that are kinda shocked to find out I'm Jewish. 'That's weird.' And [they] don't quite know what to do with me," said a Jewish man, whose family has lived in the United States for several generations and who works in information technology, laughing.[16] "You're like, all of a sudden, you're like glass, easily

---

[15] F@W_ST152, Asian American woman, age 27, social media manager/optometry technician, Muslim, interview conducted October 23, 2019.
[16] F@W_ST121, White man, age 57, information technology, Jewish, interview conducted August 29, 2019.

breakable or something. And now, we're gonna offend you or something. I'm like, 'Dude, relax. If I hadn't told you, you probably wouldn't
have known.' . . . It's just new and weird and different, and they don't
know what to do with you."

As our American culture continues to fracture along racial, political, religious, regional, and gender lines, as Christians it is easy for
us to see ways in which others are not seeing our full humanity or not
giving us the benefit of the doubt due to various aspects of our own
identity. But perhaps the best way to make a difference is by first becoming aware of the ways that *others* are also experiencing the impact
of their own deeply held beliefs and then working toward positive
change for everyone. There are many things that we as Christians can
do—*and even have a responsibility to do*—to protect the rights of non-
Christians in the workplace, born out of a radical commitment to the
imago Dei.

Speak out against comments or behaviors that are critical of someone's religious practices or beliefs, whether these comments are directed at you or at someone else. As one Black pastor tells his congregants, "Don't let anyone put you down. We're all made by the same
God."[17] Seek out opportunities to discuss religious experiences with
workers of other faiths in the workplace with the purpose of learning
about and improving their experiences in the workplace rather than
only sharing your Christian faith. Recognize the ways in which faith
overlaps with other individual characteristics such as race and gender,
and that those who are marginalized for one identity (such as their
race or gender) are also more likely than other groups to be marginalized because of religious identity. If you have an organizational
leadership role, sensitively find ways to inquire about workers from
other faiths and try to discern what those in your organization might
need. Workplaces leaders should especially look out to ensure that

---

[17]F@W_Pastor Interview (PA)_18, Black man, age 72, pastor, evangelical, interview conducted
June 2, 2020.

those from minority groups are treated fairly and equitably regarding religious expression and accommodation in the workplace.

REFLECTION QUESTIONS

For everyone

- What would it look like in your workplace for every person, regardless of their beliefs or identity, to be viewed with value and dignity? Are there ways your organization could do this better?

- What are the religious norms in your occupation or particular workplace? How might these norms affect how the religion (or nonreligion) of individual workers is viewed by others?

- Have you seen circumstances in the workplace where Christians are discriminated against in ways that might be consequential for them professionally? If so, what are the factors that contribute to this?

- In your workplace, are Christians from some demographic groups (like racial minorities) more likely than those from other groups to experience discrimination?

- How might you contribute to an environment where it is safe to talk about religion in a way that supports, not undermines, organizational goals? How might you use the power you have to speak out against discrimination or make the workplace experience better for others?

- Are there ways that certain workplace activities, rules, or expectations might conflict with someone's religious beliefs? How can you support better religious accommodations for everyone with respect to religious appearance, observance, and expression?

For faith communities

- If you are a church or parachurch leader, how could you create room to discuss how those from different religious backgrounds may be marginalized at work because of their faith, even if they are not treated in an overtly discriminatory way?

- How do you think Christians should engage with those from different religious backgrounds in their workplaces? How are you encouraging or modeling this kind of engagement?

6

FOCUSING ON INDIVIDUAL RESPONSIBILITY

*He holds success in store for the upright, he is a
shield to those whose walk is blameless.*

PROVERBS 2:7

OUR FRIEND JEREMY, an accountant, told us his company encouraged him and other employees to round up their hours, billing for
more time than they had actually worked. Uncomfortable with this
dishonesty, Jeremy felt convicted by his faith to bill only for the hours
he had actually worked. But he kept his motivations and actions private
from his coworkers, believing it was more spiritual to do so.

In our survey, 96 percent of people who have a religious tradition told
us they behave ethically at work—a number that, somewhat surprising
to us, does not differ appreciably among the nonreligious. In short, nearly
everyone thinks they are being ethical at work. But Christians like Jeremy
are more likely to attach this moral compass to their faith. Christians
often feel their faith leads to a deep sense of personal ethical responsibility that influences how they do their work, whether they are honest,
and how they treat others, even if they never actually tell people that it is
their faith that is acting as a moral compass. Indeed, among those who

attend religious services regularly, 80 percent say that the habits they have learned from their faith community help them succeed at work.

What do Christians mean when they talk about the importance of personal responsibility for ethical behavior at work? In our interviews with Christians from a variety of workplaces, they tended to talk about it in two main ways: avoiding what is wrong and doing what is right. First, they expressed concerns about engaging in or promoting immoral behaviors. It was clear that they wanted to avoid doing things at work that they viewed as contrary to God's ideals. Behaviors that were mentioned regularly included things such as fostering or engaging in intoxication, inappropriate sexual behavior, and stealing through their work. This also included what some might see as minor infractions such as personal use of office supplies or cutting corners about time. In this category our respondents also said they experienced ethical struggles around issues where there is significant disagreement among Christians about what the right course of action is, for example, when addressing issues such as abortion and LGBTQ+ communities in the workplace.

The second main way Christians saw their faith affecting their ethical behavior at work related to the importance of proactively doing what is right. In particular, we frequently heard about the importance of being honest and the ways honesty is encouraged by Christian faith. We also heard about the ways faith encourages us to work hard and help others at work.

AVOIDING IMMORALITY

Overall, more than 20 percent of the US workers we surveyed reported that they are at least occasionally expected to act in ways that contradict their faith.[1] We found that several factors influence how likely it is that these workers experienced such faith-work conflicts, including their

---

[1]We have reported these statistics elsewhere in an article. See Elaine Howard Ecklund, Denise Daniels, Daniel Bolger, and Laura Johnson, "A Nationally Representative Survey of Faith and Work: Demographic Subgroup Differences Around Calling and Conflict," *Religions* 11, no. 6 (2020): 287.

race, income level, and religious tradition. A higher proportion of Black respondents (30 percent) reported being expected to act in ways that contradicted their faith compared with White respondents (20 percent), suggesting that at least some experiences of faith-work conflict are more common for workers who are Black. Our research supports the idea that one's faith both changes the expectations one has of oneself and makes one more aware of discrepancies between one's personal values and the expectations of one's work.

Those who have felt that they are expected to act in ways that contradict their religious beliefs at work by racial group

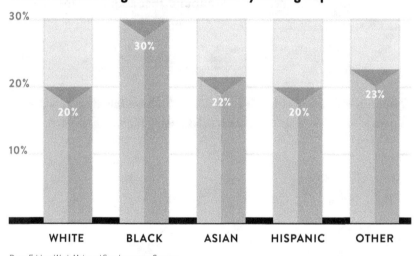

Data: Faith at Work Main and Supplementary Surveys

Figure 6.1

Our research shows that race, income, and religious tradition may all correlate with employees' level—and therefore power—in their organization. Workers at lower levels in the organization may be more likely to face requests that conflict with their sense of right and wrong. Another possibility is that the characteristics of race (particularly among those who are Black), income level (low), and religious tradition (for Christians generally but evangelicals in particular), may influence the extent to which employees are attuned to and aware of conflicts between their own moral code and the demands of the organization they work for. Those who are most marginalized at work may be the ones who take their faith the most seriously in terms of practices. In other words, those who tend to be most marginalized may also be most cognizant of situations that have moral components to them. It is also possible that something about one or more of these characteristics of race, income, and faith tradition may create distinct or higher expectations of a person's own behavior, (feeling like one needs to act as a representative for one's group, for example), making it more likely for there to be a discrepancy between what the workplace is asking of them and what their faith demands. We found that about a third of evangelicals were likely to experience dissonance between their faith and workplace demands, which was significantly higher than any other religious group.

Respondents across religious traditions who have felt that they are expected to act in ways that contradict their religious beliefs at work

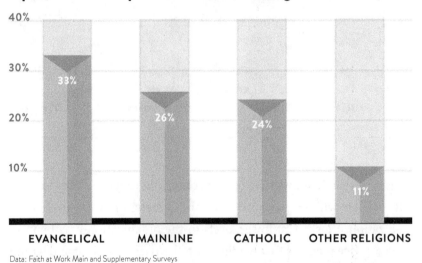

EVANGELICAL   MAINLINE   CATHOLIC   OTHER RELIGIONS

Data: Faith at Work Main and Supplementary Surveys

Figure 6.2

Those Christians we interviewed about personal ethics at work talked a lot about making sure they promoted moral behaviors, did not engage in immoral behaviors (even in their hearts), and that, under certain conditions, even vetted the moral behaviors of others. They reported pressure to engage in workplace behaviors that conflicted with their personal moral codes, things such as cutting corners, stealing or misusing the property of others, or viewing sexualized images. They told us that when they noticed something that was out of alignment with their moral code, their faith gave them the strength to stand up to an authority figure or client as a result of their desire, as several of those we interviewed put it, "to live a life of integrity."

When we followed up to learn more about their experiences with faith-work conflict, Christians in a variety of fields spoke about how their faith conflicted with potentially immoral things they were asked to do in the workplace and spent a lot of time reflecting on what constitutes immoral behavior at work. They almost always described behaviors such as becoming intoxicated or viewing pornography as examples of immoral behavior they tried to avoid. For example, a Christian investment strategist from Georgia told his bosses that he had to opt out of working on a beer account because of his Christian convictions and thankfully "they didn't push back."[2] In chapter two we met a graphic artist who told us that his faith has influenced the "direction I go into with my art."[3] He explained that he refuses certain kinds of contracts because of his faith, particularly those for projects that would promote pot dispensaries or strip clubs.

An evangelical criminal investigator discussed the personal moral responsibility his faith compels him to uphold and how that affects his work with sexual abuse cases.[4] "Sometimes, there's certain language that I have to use, because I'm reiterating something verbatim, that is uncomfortable. Certain times, there's things that involve pornography

---

[2]F@W_ST140, Black man, age 37, investment strategist, evangelical, interview conducted October 1, 2019.
[3]F@W_ST43, Black man, age 48, graphic artist, evangelical, interview conducted January 29, 2019.
[4]F@W_ST49, Black man, age 38, criminal investigator, evangelical, interview conducted February 6, 2019.

that is required for me to be involved with and that is uncomfortable," he said.

> I try to check myself [laughs nervously] and make sure that I'm not just using this as a cover to indulge in something that I really want to do but should not do. So, there's a lot of introspection that goes on ahead of time, and then just putting it in the appropriate context is helpful as well. It's important that I relay what this person said because it could hurt somebody, or somebody has been hurt by them. And I need to do this because this is somebody's daughter that's been exploited, and I need to help them in whatever way I can, even if it means viewing something that I don't ordinarily view.

As you can tell by this mental back and forth, this criminal investigator reflected a lot on his internal motivations about various tasks his job required.

Christian workers also told us that their views on personal immoral behaviors sometimes came into conflict with the rights of others, with the norms of the workplace, and even with legal structures. Current social issues were top of mind for many Christians, abortion and LGBTQ+ rights in particular (using their faith to adopt stances of either for or against). This was not surprising, given these are some of the most contentious social issues of our day, yet we were struck both by the consistency of the themes that arose over and over and by what was *not* included. For example, we rarely heard about struggles Christian workers faced in their efforts to avoid gossip, greed, envy, or the many other sinful behaviors related to personal responsibility, which the Bible and church teachings explore more explicitly and to which Christians historically have been attentive. It seems that our respondents were mainly reacting *against* changing cultural norms and values rather than *asserting* cultural norms and values based on core Christian ethical frameworks.

Many Christians we spoke with discussed how important it was for them to align their faith with their approach to abortion and LGBTQ+ issues, and how difficult it was to do so at times. In addition, some Christians were especially conflicted because they felt other Christians sometimes used these two issues as a litmus test for who had a genuine Christian faith. Evangelical Christians, especially, talked about how these issues created significant tensions for them. Sometimes they did not know how to be true to their faith while also following workplace norms and in some cases legal requirements such as nondiscrimination laws when hiring. Mainly, they just expressed struggle. They often discussed their internal conflict, concluding with a lack of certainty about what their responsibility was in morally charged situations where they did not have decision-making power.

"There was one time where we had a case where a child had been raped, and it was a disabled child, and as a result of this rape she became pregnant, and I know that there were some discretionary funds that were used to fund her abortion," a man who works in child services told us, describing the tension he experienced around this case.[5] "You know, it was just an awful situation. I felt uneasy about the whole thing, . . . [that she had experienced violence] and using public funds to pay for this girl's abortion, I felt very uneasy, . . . uncomfortable about the whole thing." A woman who works as a nurse said there had "never been abortion procedures where I worked. But [if there had been] that would've been an issue where I would not have been able to participate in that."[6] Unsurprisingly, several Christians who work in the medical profession spoke about abortion, saying they would be unable to work somewhere that conducted, condoned, or participated in abortions in any way because of a broader Christian ethic to protect what they see as the beginning of life.

Talking with us about the tension in her school around some LGBTQ+ issues, a teacher told us she felt that "there's a weird mixture of some of these issues between what your religious beliefs are, and

---

[5] F@W_ST171, White man, age 35, child services specialist, evangelical, interview conducted December 6, 2019.

[6] F@W_ST98, White woman, age 60, registered nurse, evangelical, interview conducted July 10, 2019.

what you believe the laws of nature are, and [workplace guidelines]."[7] A program manager discussed struggling with an in-depth diversity training because of "my Christian beliefs when we get to all the sexual orientation material." He continued,

> But I know that there's laws and everything that I have to live within, re-
> gardless of what I believe. And what may happen in my church is separate
> from . . . what this government that has control says. And I don't personally
> try to discriminate against a person because I don't really have the right to
> discriminate. But the belief of whether it's right or wrong is—that's the struggle.[8]

Others struggled in different ways to align their Christian faith with issues related to sexual orientation.

A woman who works as a Spanish teacher told us that she uses her faith at work to be especially accepting of people who are sexual minorities.[9] She said that her faith helps her to be especially "nonjudgmental. I believe that there's just one judge. I'm very open minded. I'm not conservative or fundamental." She explained, "In my former marriage, I was married to a fundamentalist, where it was just like I had family members who are homosexual, friends that are homosexual. And when I would talk with them, he would be like, 'Okay. You can't get close to them, because what they're doing is immoral.' And I'm like, 'No, I don't believe that at all.'" This approach carried over to her work as well. She mentioned, "I was the adviser for the LGBTQ+ Club at my high school. And the kids didn't know that I was a Christian. All they knew is that I am a loving person and someone that they could go to and confide in. . . . But in there [with the students] I saw this as a spiritual calling, as a way of influencing my students."

Often those who are not in agreement with a majority Christian view feel like others call their faith into question, and this makes it stressful

---

[7]F@W_ST78, White man, age 28, teacher, Catholic, interview conducted June 3, 2019.
[8]F@W_ST09, Black man, age 50, program manager, evangelical, interview conducted November 2, 2018.
[9]F@W_ST190, White woman, age 45, high school teacher, evangelical, interview conducted January 21, 2020.

for them at work. For example, a man who directs field operations for a farm said he expresses his faith at work through how he shows love to others:

> If you express God as the personification of love, and I'm not talking about, you know, just touchy, feely love, but the kind of love that edifies and encourages and builds people up, and that kind of love that heals people, the kind of love that, you know, tells the world hey, I'm your friend, I'm going to come alongside you, I'm going to help you any way I can, I'm not here to condemn you or judge you. . . . Then I really think if that's what you're expressing and it's a true form of God, I'm not sure that you can do that enough.[10]

He explained that sometimes the problem at his workplace becomes when there are

> certain denominations of Christianity that, for instance, tell gays that they're not saved or who tell women that you have a specific role, that you're not suited to do certain things within the church. And to me that's where the wheels begin to come off the cart. It isn't so much the fact that you're expressing faith in God, but how are you doing it, and what message are you sending? And that may be a little bit nebulous, I don't know, but that's about the best way that I can describe it.

While we heard from a number of Christians who struggled in the face of a mismatch between their faith values and the values and expectations of their workplace, they were somewhat unusual. The majority of Christian workers across denominations and traditions did not struggle with any kind of disconnect between their own values and the values of their workplace, in part because they actively separate their faith from their work. They rarely thought about how their faith might be contributing to tensions they feel toward the norms of their workplace, instead choosing to simply prioritize those norms. Indeed, it was common to talk with Christian workers who had never thought about ways their faith might play a role at work.

---

[10]F@W_ST58, White man, age 63, director of field operations and owner of farm-management company, evangelical, interview conducted February 22, 2019.

DO THE RIGHT THING

While some Christians we interviewed spoke about ways that they were avoiding what they felt were immoral or unethical behaviors in the workplace, others talked about ways their faith motivated them to "do the right thing" at work. In his book *God and Mammon*, sociologist Robert Wuthnow writes, "In the labor force as a whole about one person in three chooses 'always trying to be honest' as the best definition of ethics when presented with a list of five alternatives. Among those who attend religious services every week, this proportion is even higher, rising to about four people in ten."[11] Our research bears this out. Those we interviewed placed a particular emphasis on the importance of telling the truth at work, and quite a few people we talked with shared the internal conflicts that arose when they were asked to lie to benefit or cover up for themselves or someone else.

A woman who works in a university told us about a situation where she felt her sense of honesty conflicted with the expectations of her colleagues.[12] "There was one time [another] faculty member was insisting that a student had completed his minor, and the student was lacking a unit, and the faculty member was saying, 'Well, I've signed off on it so it's OK,'" she recalled. "And I was saying no, it's not. I cannot possibly grant the student the minor because he hasn't earned the right amount of units." Not only did she feel that granting the student the minor would be against her values, but "definitely, that would be going against my faith as well," she explained, "cause it's just fundamentally dishonest."

In situations where they were not able to do the right thing, some of our respondents told us about difficult decisions they had to make about their own career prospects. A maintenance technician said at his previous job, he "was starting to be asked to do things more frequently

---

[11]See Robert Wuthnow, *God and Mammon in America* (New York: Free Press, 1994), 111.
[12]F@W_ST103, White woman, age 57, teacher and librarian, mainline, interview conducted July 18, 2019.

that were what I would consider unethical and not right. Be dishonest on paperwork or fudge numbers even on timesheets to try to cut employees down, and I refused. And instead of being fired, I—well, I submitted my resignation."[13]

In addition to wanting to be honest and tell the truth in their workspaces, many of these Christians also talked about the importance of working hard and helping others at work as a function of their faith. In some ways, these outward expressions of doing the right thing might also be viewed as an extension of honesty. Lance Morrow, a renowned American essayist, writes that most people view honesty only as "not telling a bald-faced lie." In contrast, he argues that an "honest employee is one who works hard, never engages in 'time theft' by taking undue breaks, and avoids 'energy theft' of the kind that might result from being emotionally or mentally distracted."[14]

Among the Christians we interviewed, we found this broader approach to honesty, perhaps drawing on a Christian history that establishes a relationship between religion and hard work. "I think my faith definitely affects my work," a scientist who works in a lab told us, "because I think I am going to do the best I can, every time, for everybody. And I think that's more faith-based than it is just job responsibility. I think I want to go a little bit beyond what the job responsibility is and try to do my best and be the best example that I can be."[15] A woman who works in information technology at a university also explained that her faith motivates her to work hard. "I try to be the person who does what I say I'm going to do, that I'm reliable," she said.[16] "I have cultivated a culture of 'yes' in my world. If people come and ask me to

---

[13]F@W_ST44, White man, age 31, maintenance technician, evangelical, interview conducted January 30, 2019.

[14]Lance Morrow, *God and Mammon: Chronicles of American Money* (New York: Encounter Books, 2020).

[15]F@W_ST90, White man, age 64, clinical laboratory scientist, evangelical, interview conducted June 26, 2019.

[16]F@W_ST07, White woman, age 49, senior communications specialist in university information technology, mainline, interview conducted October 31, 2018.

do something, I figure out how to say yes. I might not be able to do it exactly the way they want it, exactly when they want it, but I work to make people feel like working with me is easy." (This "culture of saying yes" as a way to display one's faith was particularly gendered, with women being more likely than men to say that they felt compelled to respond to work demands because of their faith, a point we will return to in a later chapter.) Because of their faith, these Christian workers are not telling those around them that they are working hard. Instead, they hope that others will "just notice" their work and ask them "for the hope that is within me" (see 1 Peter 3:15-16), as a plurality of Christians quipped as they referred to the biblical passage. Their bottom line was to work hard and with integrity in part to set a moral example for others.

While very few people actually quoted Scripture in our interviews, a few themes from Scripture seemed to permeate their thoughts about work. In his letter to the Colossians, Paul writes, "Whatever you do, work at it with all your heart, as working for the Lord, not for human masters" (Colossians 3:23). Many Christians we interviewed seemed to resonate with this idea. They talked about the value of hard work, thrift, and efficiency in their work and connected this to their faith. Some of them viewed their efforts at work as a response to God's grace, and a few even said that hard work is a way of proving faith, seemingly reflecting the apostle James's statement, "I will show you my faith by my deeds" (James 2:18).

When Christians were not able to perform at their best or work their hardest, they often felt guilty. For example, a program manager said he feels like sometimes he's "slothing off a little bit, right. I know that [work is] due, I got two days to do it, and maybe you wait until the last minute, so you put something together, but then you realize, eh, it probably wasn't my best effort."[17] At times like this, his Christian faith brings him back to his core values. He spoke as if to remind himself of

---

[17]F@W_ST09, Black man, age 50, program manager, evangelical, interview conducted November 2, 2018.

how he wanted to view his job and his personal effort at work, saying, "It's the job you have. You were given this job. It allows you to support your family and therefore to reflect Christ. We should be always giving our best. Do everything to the best of your ability and then let everything else—it'll work itself out." Christians often spoke of their faith leading to a sense of guilt when they could not work at maximum pace because they were completely maxed out, as so many were during the pandemic because of increased childcare responsibilities alongside work.

Christian workers we interviewed also talked about God keeping them accountable to doing their best work. A woman who works in the accounting department of her company told us God

is the one that sees whether I do right or wrong, and when I review my accounts, I can half do them, or I can do them to the best of my ability and God can be my witness. But everything I do, I do it knowing that God sees and knows everything. And he knows my heart, whether I'm putting my heart into it or whether I'm kind of going behind the line and not doing what I should do like being on time and just, you know, just demonstrating Christlike behavior in the workplace.[18]

The graphic designer we quoted previously told us, "I always try to think, when I do a job, I try not to think of it as I'm doing it for a client, I'm doing it for God. So, that sort of inspires me to do my best."[19]

WHAT CONGREGANTS WANT FROM FAITH LEADERS

In general, Christian workers we interviewed want to hear their pastors and other faith leaders talk more about how Christians should act at work and how they can develop a personal ethical approach that is consistent with their faith. Yet, hearing a faith leader talk directly about workplace issues, especially issues involving personal ethical responsibility, is relatively rare. It was striking to us how few of our survey respondents remembered having heard their faith leaders ever talk about

---

[18]F@W_ST71, Black woman, age 66, reimbursement analyst, evangelical, interview conducted May 28, 2019.

[19]F@W_ST43, Black man, age 48, graphic artist, evangelical, interview conducted January 29, 2019.

these issues. Only 16 percent of practicing Christians said their faith leaders often or very often discuss how congregants should behave at work. For those who identified as evangelical Christians, 28 percent said their faith leaders often or very often have these discussions; for mainline Protestant Christians it was only 12 percent, and for Catholics only 7 percent. It should not surprise us that Christians who attend services more often are more likely to say they have heard discussions about faith at work. Among those who attend religious services multiple times a week, 41 percent have heard their faith leaders talk about how to behave at work, while less than 5 percent of those who attend only several times per year have heard faith leaders talk about this topic. It was also slightly more common for younger Christian workers we spoke with to say they had heard about faith at work from a faith leader, with 18 percent of those ages eighteen to thirty-four saying their faith leader discusses how to behave at work often or very often.[20]

One of the reasons Christian communities lack discussion of faith and personal ethical responsibility at work could be that pastors lack experience with the work environments and struggles that many working people face.[21] The Christians we spoke with suggested that they want their spiritual leaders to understand their work but often experienced a miss from their pastors. "I think, unfortunately, very few pastors have been in the work world. And I think it's hard to relate," said an evangelical man who worked as an actuary.[22]

> I know pastors have very demanding lives because of what they do, but in a lot of ways their schedules are pretty flexible. That same thing is not true for many of those in the work world. And so, I've definitely seen situations with

---

[20]For more on what congregants want from their faith leaders, see Elaine Howard Ecklund, Denise Daniels, and Rachel C. Schneider, "From Secular to Sacred: Bringing Work to Church," *Religions* 11, no. 9 (2020): 442.

[21]See F@W_ST103, White woman, age 57, teacher/librarian, mainline, interview conducted July 18, 2019; F@W_ST96, White man, age 50, actuary, evangelical, interview conducted July 3, 2019; F@W_ST87, White man, age 35, farmer, evangelical, interview conducted June 14, 2019; F@W_ST81, Black man, age 69, concierge, evangelical, interview conducted June 5, 2019.

[22]F@W_ST96, White man, age 50, actuary, evangelical, interview conducted July 3, 2019.

what I'd say [is] a lack of empathy or understanding toward just how demanding work can be. And I don't know that a lot of pastors realize that. I
mean, I think intellectually they know it, but I don't think they get it.

From our interviews with Christian workers, we have identified
practices we believe would help church leaders address faith-at-work
topics with their congregants, especially those involving personal
ethical responsibility. At their core, these practices require curiosity
and a listening posture about different types of jobs across a range of
industries and workplaces. Pastors could prioritize reaching out to congregants whose jobs they are least familiar with to learn about what
these workers experience on a regular basis. They could also ask congregants about the specific tasks, interactions, joys, struggles, challenges, and fears associated with various kinds of work.

Provide targeted ethical support. Some Christians we spoke with
felt church leaders could do more to provide guidance and support for
workers in professions in which they are likely to face difficult circumstances and ethical struggles. Our Christian respondents mentioned
that those who work in law enforcement, health care, or as firefighters—
anyone who sees what one called "the ugly side of . . . the human
species"—might need more help with personal ethical reflection. As
this man who works in the Department of Corrections explained,
"There are professions that are a little bit more strenuous than others
in that sense," and those in such professions may need additional
support in integrating faith and work.[23]

Provide workplace groups. Christian workers told us that churches
could offer tailored small groups for members who work in the same
field and thus would better understand the specific challenges and
ethical dilemmas they may face in the workplace due to their faith. These
groups could provide a kind of counter-discourse, a knowledgeable,
alternative way of talking about things that subverts the dominant

---

[23]See F@W_ST25, Hispanic man, age 36, asset manager, Department of Corrections, Catholic,
interview conducted December 7, 2018.

discourse. Such groups would reflect a range of occupations, such as veterans, first responders, service workers, business owners, government workers, medical professionals, working parents, and educators.[24] If a given church is not large enough for such specific occupational groupings, perhaps they could be developed across multiple churches in a given area or through the support of parachurch organizations.

Visit church members at work. One final recommendation is for clergy to visit church members in their workplaces, something Elaine's current pastor often does. This would allow church leaders to better understand a range of job experiences as well as the workplace ethical issues their congregants sometimes face. It could also help Christian workers see connections between their work and their faith. "I think the immersion [is important] because what happens is we try to stratify church and home and work and school. . . . So, we have all these silos that we're tryin' to hop from place to place to place, but if we're able to kind of intermingle, it would help a lot," said a criminal investigator we interviewed.[25] He liked the idea of church leaders visiting workplaces and the possibility of creating a more radical integration of work and church.

REFLECTION QUESTIONS

For everyone

- Have you experienced situations in which your faith commitments were at odds with workplace demands in ways that made you feel ethically squeamish? If so, what made you see the discrepancies between your faith and the situation at hand? If not,

---

[24]F@W_ST40, White man, age 42, paramedic supervisor, evangelical, interview conducted January 17, 2019; F@W_ST45, White woman, age 48, tutor, evangelical, interview conducted January 30, 2019; F@W_ST56, Asian woman, age 35, pediatrician, evangelical, interview conducted February 20, 2019; F@W_ST77, White woman, age 22, data analyst, evangelical, interview conducted June 3, 2019; F@W_ST37, White/Hispanic man, age 43, high school ROTC instructor, evangelical, interview conducted January 10, 2019.

[25]F@W_ST49, Black man, age 38, criminal investigator, evangelical, interview conducted February 6, 2019.

do you think you have a particularly healthy workplace, or is it possible you are not as attentive to ethical conflicts between your faith and work as you could be?

- What are some ways that Christians could or should approach situations in which personal faith-based responsibilities and professional responsibilities might be at odds? When is it appropriate to stay in a situation and try to change it, and when is it better to leave a situation?

- To what extent have you seen examples of where an emphasis on personal integrity blinds a person to how their decisions and actions can affect the opportunities and outcomes of others?

- Are there certain moral issues that you think Christians ought to be raising in workplaces like yours?

For faith communities

- What are the moral and ethical issues that are most commonly discussed in your church? Are these issues ones that you experience in your workplace?

- Is your church more likely to talk about personal responsibility and individual sin or more likely to talk about systems of sin? How does your church's view of sin shape how you see workplace ethics?

7

FOCUSING ON SYSTEMS THINKING

When you reap the harvest of your land, do not reap to the very edges of your field or gather the gleanings of your harvest. Do not go over your vineyard a second time or pick up the grapes that have fallen. Leave them for the poor and the foreigner.

LEVITICUS 19:9-10

YOU ARE LISTENING to music on headphones as you step into an empty elevator. If you are having a good day, you might dance around a bit when the doors close—after all, no one is watching. Now imagine that you get into a packed elevator. You and the group of strangers you are riding with know exactly what is expected: face the doors, only fleeting eye contact, no talking. Sociologist Erving Goffman had a field day with this elevator scenario. He used to send his students out to violate our unspoken elevator norms to see what happened. We dare you to try it sometime!

As research in organizational behavior has shown for the past one hundred years, people act differently in groups than they do when alone. This recognition of the power of groups to shape behavior has led to the development of systems thinking, a holistic approach to understanding the influence and interactions of the components of a system rather than trying to understand each part by itself. In short, a social system is the product of the interactions of its parts, not just the sum of its parts. As we saw in the last chapter, many Christians have deeply internalized messages about the importance of their own behaviors as a way of honoring God but do not often recognize how the systems they are a part of not only shape them but also affect others. It turns out that systems matter. It is very difficult to act outside of the norms that shape behaviors when we are part of a strong social system, as Goffman's students learned.[1]

Elaine experienced this firsthand when she moved to Texas to work at Rice University and joined her current church. The pastor graduated from Texas A&M, and she quickly learned that graduates of the school make a "whoop" sound whenever the name of their university is mentioned. Many times over the past fifteen years, when someone who graduated from A&M mentioned their university, she too made the "whoop" sound without even thinking about it—just because everyone else was doing it. When patterns of behavior become regularized in certain kinds of situations, the idea of institutions is developed. An institution can be brick and mortar (such as a school building), and it can be made up of symbols and norms (such as raising one's hand in a class when one has a question). Institutions and organizations shape how people think, act, and relate to each other within a particular kind of setting. For example, the institution of education regulates the kinds of behaviors we expect in a school setting. We might expect to see students sitting in chairs facing a teacher who is in the front of the group when we enter a classroom. And if a particular school has a mascot of a bear, then even years after a student graduates, certain feelings and practices are elicited whenever she sees that symbolic mascot. In her book *How Institutions Think*, the

---

[1]See Michael Hviid Jacobsen and Soren Kristiansen, "Goffman's Sociology of Everyday Life Interaction," in *The Social Thought of Erving Goffman* (Los Angeles: Sage, 2014), 67-84.

great anthropologist Mary Douglas argues that institutions take on a life of their own, so much so that people often do things expected by their institutions without necessarily having a good reason for it, like Elaine's whoop!

Institutionalized expectations can be good or bad. On the one hand, Douglas believes the healthiest institutions build ways of thinking and doing that foster cooperation and altruism.[2] If we change how things are done in an institution such as the law or education, then we have the possibility to change the behavior of the organizations and the individuals that are part of that institution. On the other hand, there are times when systems can embed and perpetuate *ways of doing things* that create an unfair playing field that even the most well-intentioned individuals replicate just because they are part of the institution and that's the way we do things here. In these situations, the people who are part of these systems may not even be aware that they are taking part in something that might be hurting others.

People sometimes participate in racial and religious epithets without even knowing they are participating. For example, it was not until she became an adult that Denise realized the phrase "I've been gypped," which she'd heard and used regularly throughout her childhood to communicate an experience of being cheated, was a denigration of the Roma people group, deriving from their colloquial name of "Gypsy" (a term itself that is viewed as a racial slur).[3] If people become aware of the hidden meanings of these phrases and how they make whole groups of people feel, then individuals might have the ability to stand against institutionalized ways of doing things and stop using them. Many feel, however, that they have no power to make things better. And most people, we find, do not ponder the institutions and systems they are a part of. They are not aware of how these systems can shape

---

[2]Mary Douglas, *How Institutions Think* (Syracuse, NY: Syracuse University Press, 1986).
[3]"Defining Anti-Roma Racism," US Department of State, www.state.gov/defining-anti-roma -racism/.

individual choices or how, under certain conditions, individuals might have the ability to change systems![4]

We found that Christian workers tend to focus on personal morality rather than the moral weight of workforce systems. When they do become aware of the impact of systems, they do not see how they can use their Christian faith to bring changes. But we believe that because they are often in positions imbued with power, Christians who are leaders in their organizations have a particular responsibility to understand the systems in which they are embedded and to use their power to bring changes when these systems create problems for some individuals or groups of people.[5]

Engaging in systems thinking is especially important for Christians because Christianity is a corporate faith. It is about a community. Scripture talks extensively about the community of God's people and God relating to his community. In the Old Testament the Hebrew people collectively experience consequences—positive and negative—of individuals' behaviors. In the New Testament we see Jesus' emphasis on the importance of the church (see Matthew 16:18), and the apostle Paul regularly emphasizes the body/community of Christ and the community of believers. In the Western world we have tended to overlook the scriptural emphasis on community by fostering a deeper commitment to individualism than the corporate demands of the faith. Partly because it is easier and partly because in US culture we prioritize the individual over the community, we as Western Christians more often put the individual person rather than the group at the center of our thinking. This makes it harder for us to conceive of ourselves as part of a community or to think of ourselves as having responsibility to

---

[4]See Monty L. Lynn, Michael J. Naughton, and Steve VanderVeen, "Connecting Religion and Work: Patterns and Influences of Work-Faith Integration," *Human Relations* 64, no. 5 (2010): 675-701.

[5]See, for example, Jim Herrington, Trisha Taylor, and R. Robert Creech, *The Leader's Journey: Accepting the Call to Personal and Congregational Transformation* (Grand Rapids, MI: Baker Academic, 2020). We have learned so much about how to apply systems thinking to organizational leadership from this book and from *The Leader's Journey Podcast*.

those beyond ourselves and our close family or friends. One way we can see this in our data is in response to the statement, "Anyone can find a good job if they try hard enough." Those who agree with this statement tend to focus on the power of the individual over the system. Yet, we know that sometimes no matter how hard someone tries, there are factors that prevent a person from succeeding in a given situation. It is perhaps not surprising that Christians are more likely than those from other religions to agree with this statement. Evangelical Christians are the most likely of all.

Respondents who agree that anyone can find a good job if they try hard enough

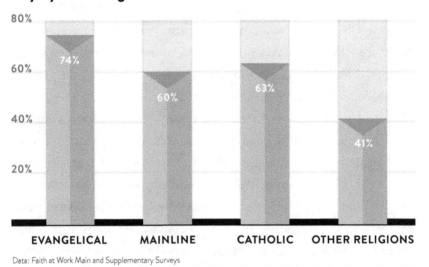

Data: Faith at Work Main and Supplementary Surveys

Figure 7.1

MOVING FROM INDIVIDUAL TO CORPORATE RESPONSIBILITY

In the Bible, we see God attending to the importance of systems. God commands his people to prioritize others beyond their own social or ethnic group. In both the Bible and broader Christian teachings, there are repeated examples of how to care for the poor. These mandates are typically not focused on an *individual's* responsibility to care for those in need but rather are injunctions for *whole groups* of people to care for those in other groups—especially those who were the most impoverished and at risk (often the widows and orphans at that time). The Old Testament law required landowning Israelites to leave food for the poor as a part of their agriculture practice: "When you reap the harvest of your land, do not reap to the very edges of your field or gather the gleanings of your harvest. Do not go over your vineyard a second time or pick up the grapes that have fallen. Leave them for the poor and the foreigner" (Leviticus 19:9-10).

Part of the tithe in the Old Testament was allocated by the Levites to those in need (Deuteronomy 14:28-29). Similarly, we see in the New Testament the responsibility of the community of faith to care for the poor through their collective activity. In Acts 6, a group of Greek followers of Christ were tasked with daily distribution of food to the widows among them. And in his first letter to Timothy, Paul outlines the responsibility the church has to widows who are in need (1 Timothy 5).

WE ARE WARY OF SYSTEMS THINKING

Yet, we often encounter pushback to the idea of systems thinking, particularly in some Christian circles. There are several reasons for this. First, systems thinking requires a lot of thought and reflection, and changing systems takes more time than individual actions. It is harder for many, for example, to be part of large-scale efforts to address poverty in a city or to change how large-scale institutions such as the government respond to poverty than it is to give some spare change to a homeless person we meet on the street. Doing something positive for a particular person also makes us feel like we are making a difference in the moment, unlike efforts to change the structures that contribute to poverty, where the results are far from immediate. While there can be immense value in individual acts of kindness, individual acts often are simply not as powerful or as lasting as systemic change. Our faith can help us have the courage to undertake more long-term efforts. A Hispanic woman working as a senior program manager explained that her faith "helps [with] both coping and [as] a change agent. . . . You need to be able to cope with things because you can't just change things overnight. And I think [faith] also gives you patience that, over time, things can change, by the effect that you can bring to a place." Faith can provide the long view in an organization and a recognition that while change may not happen immediately, we are responsible to God and to our communities for playing a role in the story of change, even if we are not ultimately responsible for the outcome.

A second reason that some Christians are resistant to systems thinking is that it is viewed as political. They assume that efforts focused on addressing systems are driven by a particular political ideology rather than recognizing a systemic approach as, at its core, consistent with a Christian ethic. Thinking and acting systemically in life is consistent with biblical teaching.

Finally, thinking about how we are part of systems much bigger than ourselves can be intimidating and overwhelming. We often do not know what we can or should do to influence these systems, nor do we have a Christian imagination for how God might want to use us to change them. Thus, we buy into American individualism rather than Christian community. We shift our attention to things that are more obviously under our control. In the workplace, we tend to focus our efforts on our own personal behaviors and ignore the social systems in which our individual behaviors are embedded.

From our research, we have uncovered three ways that Christian workers are using their faith to recognize and change the systems in which they participate, and three ways we think Christians *could and should* use their faith to bring changes to their workplace organizational systems. Without practices to help us notice, reflect on, and change systems, we have less hope of contributing to corporate responsibility and well-being.

EMBODIED CULTURES OF CARE

When we asked Christians how their faith compelled them to make changes in the workplace, they generally spoke about how their faith compelled them not only to care about the individuals in their organizations but to create more caring and generous workplace environments as a whole. Christians in a variety of occupations prioritized being kind and caring at work and encouraging others to be so as well. We have many examples of this from the hundreds of interviews we conducted with different types of workers. A lot of efforts to change organizations started with encouraging others toward individual acts of care, which if practiced regularly add up to what we call *embodied cultures of care*. These cultures of care are marked by broad-scale practices that prioritize flourishing for everyone in the organization. Our respondents talked about the importance of encouraging and helping others, the value of engaging in relationships with people at work, and the ways that their actions influenced the moral climate of their organizations. When such behaviors are expressed consistently over time within the same organization or community, they can have a ripple effect, cultivating kinder and happier organizations.

When we asked an auto-body technician whether he uses his faith to bring changes to the body shop where he works, he said he focuses mainly on individual acts of care, using his Christian faith to bring change to his workplace "just by helping others."[6] He went on to add, "I mean, I feel good that I'm helping somebody, whether I counsel them, whether I help them fix a car" or take them out to lunch when they are "down on their luck." As evidence of trying to change his organization, he also encourages the guys he works with to focus on helping others and helps other individuals bring subtle, small changes to his organization. Although he also noted, "Not everybody reciprocates goodwill."

His focus on helping others as part of his daily work is born out of his faith. "I feel that by having faith in God and myself, I pass on good

---

[6]F@W_ST188, Hispanic man, age 53, autobody technician, Catholic, interview conducted January 13, 2020.

intentions, [and] that makes the world a better place if everybody passes on goodwill and intentions to each other," he said. He told us he discusses with his colleagues and supervisor how his emphasis on caring for others is part of his faith.

A substitute teacher told us that her faith drives her to make connections with others at work.[7] "I believe that this was the principle . . . faith-based in the sense that it's mostly about relationships," she said. "We must, must build positive relationships with students, with teachers, with administrators, with custodians, with the cafeteria ladies; it's all about building relationships." She explained that an ethic that focuses on caring for others equally will lead to a healthier workplace for all. An epidemiologist also discussed how his faith compels him to focus on the ways he interacts with others in his workplace.[8] "I really just like to see how people are doing on an individual level," he said, "and . . . my faith impacts the way I think people are more important than what we do on earth."

A man who works in administration at a credit union told us about his quest as a Christian to be a good manager.[9] He talked about how he uses his leadership position to influence the culture of his workplace through individual acts of kindness and caring. "As a manager, I try to be a good example. . . . You want to support them [employees] in their career, whatever direction they're going or however they're growing or learning," he said.

FOSTERING HONEST ORGANIZATIONS

As we discussed in the last chapter, the Christian workers we interviewed often talked about the pressure to be dishonest in their work

---

[7] F@W_ST167, Japanese woman, age 62, substitute teacher, evangelical, interview conducted December 3, 2019.

[8] F@W_ST175, Asian man, age 32, epidemiologist, evangelical, interview conducted December 11, 2019.

[9] F@W_ST10, White man, age 59, CFO of credit union, evangelical, interview conducted November 6, 2018.

as one of the most challenging demands of the workplace that conflicted with their faith. At the individual level they discussed the importance of being personally honest as one way to express their Christian faith. But some of them also talked about how they tried to change organizational systems by encouraging others to be honest, and sometimes by confronting organizational goals and structures that are inherently dishonest. When workers focus on changing a work culture to make it more honest, or when they confront an authority figure over what they perceive to be a dishonest practice or request, they are working for systemic change. The decision to enact personal moral behavior can start to change a system if the moral framework is shared with bosses, managers, or others in the organization who are in power.

For example, a man who is second in command at a logging company told us about his commitment to honesty, driven by his Christian faith, and how he stands up for his faith in the workplace.[10] He said he often has "been told to do things that I felt were dishonest" and that he will generally do whatever his boss tells him to do unless it conflicts with his faith. If he is asked to do a dishonest thing that conflicts with his faith, he tells his boss how the action is inconsistent with what his boss wants the overall ethos of the organization to be. This both highlights the logger's concern about honesty and pushes the boss to consider the ramifications of engaging in such dishonest behavior. He has noticed that there have been positive consequences of his commitment to honesty. Specifically, the landowners and foresters he works with have generally appreciated what he stands for and feel they can trust him, which he recognizes as a way that God has honored him for standing up for his faith.

A technician said that he was often asked to change numbers on paperwork at the end of the fiscal year so that "a particular salesman's

---

[10]F@W_ST33, White man, age 48, co-owner of logging company, evangelical, interview conducted January 8, 2019.

numbers or end of quarter would look better," or "to sign off that something had shipped the day before."[11] He told his superiors that he simply would not fudge the numbers. "I will not do this because first, it's dishonest; second, it's illegal," he said, explaining that his Christian faith is what compelled him to push back. We want to be clear here: Making a personal decision not to bill for more hours than you personally worked reflects personal responsibility. Speaking out and telling the boss that you are not going to fudge the numbers is a step toward systemic change.

A truck driver said that he sometimes has been told by superiors to lie to a customer to avoid complicated paperwork or to increase the bottom line.[12] When this happened, he too escalated it. "I've told my boss, I'm not going to lie to this customer," he said. "You want somebody to lie to them, it's not gonna be me."

Another man who is the director of field operations for a fruit-packing company said that he is often asked to lie as part of his work.[13] In one instance, he was told by the company owners to lie to a farmer, saying they could buy the farmer's fruit for more money than they actually could. "They told me to lie to him to keep the business because they didn't want to lose the money that they would make from packing the fruit," the director recalled. "And I refused to do it." He said, "They threatened to fire me, and I told them that then they would have to fire me because I was not going to be purposefully deceitful to this guy." He told us,

> I just knew that I was not going to step away from what my faith told me was right . . . that I was not to lie, and also I knew or trusted God enough to believe that if they did fire me that he would provide something else for me, and as it turned out, you know, they didn't fire me, and then the next

---

[11]F@W_ST44, White man, age 31, maintenance technician, evangelical, interview conducted January 30, 2019.

[12]F@W_ST48, White man, age 39, truck driver, evangelical, interview conducted February 5, 2019.

[13]F@W_ST58, White man, age 63, director of field operations, evangelical, interview conducted February 22, 2019.

year we went from having 300,000 boxes to 600,000 boxes, so that made them very happy. And actually, two of the people involved in that, that had threatened me, came up and apologized, and one of them said that they learned something about faith from [me and the way I engaged] that particular activity.

Like this worker, Christians who stood up for honesty in the workplace often had a story of how "God remained faithful" to them, they "found a way through it," or they "received some kind of blessing" because of their faithfulness to personal Christian ethical responsibility. But such outcomes often occurred only after a struggle. For example, a welding company owner who refused to give money under the table and thus lost work told us that in spite of the lost work God has always provided for him.[14] A civil engineer told us that one time her company needed her to do an analysis that required some specialized software online and she found a note that said the software should not be used for commercial purposes.[15] She mentioned this to her boss, who said that she should just use the software anyway. Her reply: "I really don't think that's OK [laughs]. . . . I just told him no." The engineer found a way to do the work without pirating the software and felt God provided her the workaround. We see the potential for contributing to systems change when people narrate why they are doing what they are doing to those around them but especially to those in power.

CULTIVATING CARE FOR THE OPPRESSED

There were a handful of Christian workers we interviewed who talked about how their faith influenced their efforts to change unjust work systems and practices, particularly those related to race and gender. Perhaps not surprisingly, many of these individuals were themselves

---

[14]F@W_ST95, White man, age 62, owner of welding company, evangelical, interview conducted July 3, 2019.
[15]F@W_ST31, White woman, age 25, civil engineer, evangelical, interview conducted December 19, 2018.

from historically marginalized groups. One of the things that was striking to us as we analyzed transcripts from our interviews was that most of those who recognized systemic impacts were people of color. While Scripture is attentive to the impacts of systems and addresses ways that communities should attend to those who are marginalized, it was unusual to hear this kind of communal or systemic language from most of our White respondents. We think this is probably because many of us who are White have much less experience being systematically discriminated against by institutional structures.

Workers who recognize that there are systems and organizational structures that affect some people differently from others and thus create inequality in the workplace sometimes then engage in efforts to change others' attitudes toward race and gender or confront broken systems by drawing on their faith.

A woman who works for the US government in homeland security told us about her tendency to mentally pause when she observes injustice at work, to gather herself and consider ways she can best stand up for others.[16] "It is difficult being an African American woman in this field, so my faith allows me to step back sometimes and remove myself from the situation," she said. She told us her faith compels her to realize how inequalities are baked into the system she works in and motivates her to stick up for the rights of others.

In a few cases, we heard from Christians who recognize the inequality in the systems at play in their organization, but rather than trying to change systems directly, they try to increase agency for those experiencing negative outcomes. For example, a Hispanic life coach told us that her ethnic identity made her "relate to the Black experience and racism in our country. And then, too, in my work, it really has made it a point for me to look toward empowering people in those disenfranchised communities, so that their recourse

---

[16]F@W_ST162, Black woman, age 38, homeland security agency, evangelical, interview conducted November 22, 2019.

is not to keep seeking assistance from the system that is hurting them."[17] In her view, "we cannot depend on *any* [with emphasis] system outside of ourselves to make our life what we want it to be. That's not how it works. So, granted, we all may need different support at different times."

Those who confronted inequality in their organization often talked about how they had to approach these issues carefully, maintaining an even keel in order to have a chance of being heard in response to systemic injustice. One Black public health executive explained how her faith helped her respond to slights and provocations she experienced at work.[18] When we asked about her own experiences of racial discrimination, she said: "The Scripture that basically comes to mind is 'Do unto others as you would have them do unto you.' . . . So, the practices that I learned and the person that I am because of my faith in God has to immediately kick in. So, instead of backlash . . . I always just stop and think about how I need to respond." She told us, "I have a saying . . . 'respond, don't react.' And so, in a response, I have to actually think through it, and a reaction, that situation is controlling me. So, the fruits of the Spirit, which include temperance, which is self-control, have to immediately kick in, basically [laughs]. It doesn't always happen, but you know, most of the time." She said, "Being Black, you don't just do things because the government says you should do them." As a Christian, she stops and prays and thinks about how what she is doing can best change systems.

A Black woman who works in cybersecurity gave a similar explanation of relying on her faith to effectively respond to gender discrimination at work.[19] She explained,

---

[17]F@W_ Supplemental Survey Taker (SUP) 6, Hispanic woman, age 40, life coach, evangelical, interview conducted October 25, 2021.

[18]F@W_SUP12, Black woman, age 47, public health executive, Black Protestant, interview conducted November 12, 2021.

[19]F@W_ST179, Black woman, age 44, cybersecurity, evangelical, interview conducted December 13, 2019.

My faith has played a huge role in that because it has just taught me that, you know what, these are human beings at the end of the day. Yes, it is considered discrimination; however, my posture and my response to what is being done is a huge factor, right, and so if I position my response appropriately and in an inspiring way to affect change, not just for myself but for other people to come, then it could be more received. But if I don't, then, you know, it could create a negative atmosphere for myself. And so, definitely, my faith has played a huge part . . . because I've seen people who walked away, like women who just left the security team just because it was too much. They couldn't deal with just how raw some of these conversations are with these men.

It is hard to make changes when "you are like the minority [as a Black woman], the minority in a huge majority pool," she said.

Advocating for change can cost those who confront inappropriate use of power in their organization. We heard from Christians who told us they had faced personal or professional repercussions for standing up for others in a way that called systems into question. A man who now works as a custodian at a Baptist church had previously worked as an office manager for a manufacturing firm.[20] He told us that work is a space where he feels it is important to practice his Christian faith but says this has led to him being "run out of my previous job because I refused to do unethical things." Despite knowing there would be potential consequences, he spoke out when a supervisor was harassing one of his female coworkers, stating that part of being a good Christian is "protecting the weak and pursuing justice." This did lead to the supervisor being dismissed, he said, "but a pattern that I had seen in the company before I had become office manager was that if you filed a report, they usually work to try to find a reason to dismiss you within a month." After this happened, he noticed that he was being tested by people in the company who were trying to find an excuse to fire him, and "within about a month . . . I was starting to be asked to do things . . . I would

---

[20]F@W_ST44, White man, age 31, custodian, Baptist, interview conducted January 30, 2021.

consider unethical and not right," he said. "Be dishonest on paperwork or fudge numbers even on timesheets to try to cut employees down, and I refused." He had no choice but to leave the
company: "I submitted my resignation, and I went in and met with
[the CEO]. . . . I handed it to the CEO and he turned and looked at
me and said, 'You can't resign, you're fired.'"

Christians in leadership positions sometimes recognized that they
had more power than those who were at lower levels in the organization to influence the workplace climate through ways they communicated their faith values. Our Black and brown Christian respondents, in particular, often felt they had special responsibilities to
change the systems they were part of or led. "As a leader, you're always
looked at. So, when you do something good, bad, or indifferent, you're
always being judged. I know really only God judges, but in the real
world, everybody judges," said a man who works as a consultant.[21]
"And so, I try to live to a high moral code and make sure that I'm being
as honest and open as I can with everyone I deal with. So, everyone I
deal with, whether it's business and in personal life, . . . they know I'm
a Christian, [and] they know that I will not put up with, you know,
profanity or racist jokes in my presence. Things of that nature I do
not allow."

OTHER WAYS CHRISTIANS CAN
INFLUENCE WORKPLACE SYSTEMS

When talking about systems thinking, there is often a deep sense that
an individual does not have the ability to change a system. We heard
this perceived lack of agency from many of those we spoke with about
structural issues. We believe, however, that there are at least three
things Christians can and should do to bring about systemic changes
in the workplace. First, we need to notice the systems that create

---

[21]F@W_ST46, White/Hispanic man, age 57, consultant/manager, mainline, interview conducted
January 30, 2019.

difficulty and pain for individuals and be honest about the true inequalities in opportunity, economic situation, geography, family support, and other factors that make it harder for some workers to succeed. This may be particularly difficult for those of us who have benefited from the ways the current systems are structured, as there may not be much motivation for change. Second, we can contribute to creating an environment at work that aligns with Christian values. Finally, each person also needs to recognize their own power to affect systems and use this power to empower others. Christians in leadership positions especially should be attentive to the ways that they can serve their workers by putting the needs of their employees before their own.

Notice the systems that create individual pain. We sometimes want to believe that everyone starts on an equal playing field. In reality, inequality is a part of all of our systems at work and is baked into our organizations and the interactions within them. We believe Christian workers can contribute to systematic change in the workplace by building relationships with coworkers and learning how others experience work, as well as what changes might help them feel more valued and supported at work. "I mean, if you have any faith in a Creator higher than yourself, then you are definitely going to want to bring out the positivity in other people, add value to someone else's life," said a Christian cybersecurity technician.[22]

Those with decision-making authority should focus on things such as scheduling issues and pay equity in their organizations. We often underestimate the extent to which Christians who are college educated and in professional roles tend to believe that people ought to be working for the love of the work. Much of the literature on calling is focused on finding work you love and are good at—but such a perspective can quickly turn into a tool for inequity, assuming that individuals who

---

[22]FW@_ST179, Black woman, age 44, cybersecurity, evangelical, interview conducted December 13, 2019.

work out of a sense of calling should be comfortable with less pay or prestige.

The variance in the work experience for those at the top and bottom of the organization should be examined. How are schedules constructed? Do people have a say in when they are working? What are the expectations for face time at the office? If there are discrepancies across organizational levels, are they a function of the real needs of the organization or a function of the power of those in a given position? If you are a leader, what would it mean to really listen to the workers being managed? Christian organizational leaders should particularly be attentive to issues of pay in their organizations. Is the compensation for those in leadership roles reasonable in light of the pay that those in entry-level positions are earning? At a minimum, their workers should not use all of their productive capacity in a job that does not allow them to meet their basic daily needs. It is not enough to collect an office pool to provide an end-of-year gift to underpaid staff without addressing the underlying need for pay that meets the needs of the employee.

Develop a culture that aligns with Christian values and faith. We believe it would help if Christians discussed both individual and systems thinking in their churches, and created a culture in which the values of the church have greater impact on what Christians do in their workplaces. Pastors and church leaders can teach their congregants what it means for faith to have systemic moral implications. Christians can also consider the ways they might explore the values of the organizations in which they work. They can ask questions about the extent to which these values match the Christian values that shape their lives. We are *not* trying to pit individual ethics against systemic ethics and say that individual ethics do not matter. Rather, we think that many Christians have ignored systemic ethics, so we are trying to provide a corrective here. In every case, *individuals* need to act in order to make systemic changes.

The best outcomes occur when individuals think through the positive impact of the ethics embedded in a given system and elevate the use of those ethics across the system. Denise once had the opportunity to talk with some employees at a company who participated in a Christian employee resource group at a well-known high-tech firm. The members of the employee resource group had spent several months reviewing the leadership values of the company and identifying the places in which these values intersected with scriptural values. Surprising to them, they found strong alignment between the company's articulated values and Christian values expressed in Scripture. While these organizational values were not always perfectly enacted or achieved, that they were clearly and publicly articulated gave these Christian employees the opportunity to speak out when they saw management behaviors that were not consistent with the stated values of the company.

Creating an environment that supports the values and faith of employees also means allowing those of other faiths to express and embrace their faith at work. "I talk a lot about inclusion because I'm part of the Inclusion Change Team that's local here in our region of the United States," said a man who works in industrial sales.[23]

> So in five or six states, we all share a team of people that we work together to drive programs and initiatives to support the overall global inclusion activities of our company. And religion is one dimension of that. . . . I'm not out using this time or these activities as a way to promote. . . Christianity. It's more to promote that you can have that relationship with whatever—however you feel fit to be a spiritual person, whether it's Buddhism or Muslim or Catholic or Judaism. Whatever those faiths are that you are. I feel that . . . my faith is something that I have, and it's something that I use and that helps me be the person that I am. And I want people to be able to be what they want to be also.

Use your power wisely. Not everyone in a work organization has or ought to have the same level of power. But Christians should think

---

[23]F@W_ST184, White man, age 50, industrial sales, Catholic, interview conducted December 18, 2019.

deeply about where they can use power wisely. Of power, Christian intellectual Andy Crouch says,

> It is a source of refreshment, laughter, joy and life—and of more power. Remove power and you cut off life, the possibility of creating something new and better in this rich and recalcitrant world. Life is power. Power is life. And flourishing power leads to flourishing life. Of course, like life itself, power is nothing—worse than nothing—without love. But love without power is less than it was meant to be. Love without the capacity to make something of the world, without the ability to respond to and make room for the beloved's flourishing, is frustrated love.[24]

Out of love for the other, wherever possible we ought to try to distribute our power out and down. We push power out when we start training those who are close to our power level about our job. In the ideal, leaders should be training those near them in the intricacies of their work even as the leaders are doing the work itself. We push power down by giving those in positions beneath our own as much autonomy and support as possible.

Many people do not recognize the power they hold, and while some of us have more power than others, everyone has at least some power, to some extent, in some situations. Elaine saw an example of this personally when her flight to Atlanta coincided with a region-wide electricity outage, trapping passengers in the airport; automatic doors were shut down, and toilets did not flush. But as one type of power was shutting down, another type of power was rising up, the ability to use personal power to deal with a crisis. The operations directors of the airlines and airport literally and understandably put their heads in their hands, unsure what to do. But Elaine then saw an enormous fleet of wheelchairs in the center of the airport—probably nearly one hundred— and the woman who led the team was calling all of the wheelchair attendants together and telling them to go out and find people who

---

[24]See Andy Crouch, *Playing God: Redeeming the Gift of Power* (Downers Grove, IL: InterVarsity Press, 2013).

needed wheelchairs and provide help. This woman was not high up in the organizational chart, but she knew the power she had to inspire dozens of workers to help where they could. As Trisha Taylor and Jim Herrington, who host *The Leader's Journey* podcast, write: "Leadership is not just about being in charge. The best leaders know how to use influence and relationships to lead up, down, and sideways in order to shape the things they care about."[25]

We have seen Christian organizational leaders be very focused on using their power to support workers who are in crisis—helping with medical costs, caring for sick family members, or providing support after natural disasters, for example. While these activities are important, it may make even more of an impact for leaders to focus on the power they have to serve their workers during the normal course of their day-to-day work. Is the workplace supportive of everyone and the work that each person does? Are some people viewed as expendable, while others have VIP status? Is financial gain valued at the expense of those doing the work? Are the benefits of a successful organization shared among all its workers, or only those at the top or who have an ownership share?

One way Christian leaders could use their power is by addressing unjust rhythms of work and rest in their organizations. This includes modeling healthy patterns for their workers and fostering systems that allow their workers to have humane work conditions that ensure they have proper rest and are not slaves to productivity. Part of the reason we expect ever-increasing productivity from ourselves and others may be that we are unwilling to acknowledge our own limitations. Or perhaps we are seeking ultimate meaning from our work. Quite frankly, both of us have struggled—and continue to struggle—with perfectionistic tendencies that see productivity as a marker of character or maybe even God's blessing. But constantly increasing performance demands

---

[25]"Leading Up and Out: Part 1," *The Leader's Journey* (podcast), September 21, 2022, https://sites .libsyn.com/119718/website/2022/09.

serve only to increase stress, particularly as such demands are extended from ourselves to others.

REFLECTION QUESTIONS

For everyone

- How much do you know about what others in your workplace value and what challenges the workplace creates? How could you find out more?

- How do the structures of your workplace influence your behaviors? Do they create equal opportunity for all? To what extent do they allow healthy patterns of work and rest?

- What systems and structures do you have the most influence over or responsibility for?

- How does your organization express values that are either consistent or inconsistent with God's kingdom, even though the values may not be described in those terms? How might you reinforce values that are consistent with Scripture and Christian teaching? Are there ways you can address values that are inconsistent with Scripture?

- What are two things you can try in your workplace to notice and alleviate pain resulting from workplace systems? How can your community keep you accountable? How can you reflect on the effectiveness of your steps?

For faith communities

- How familiar are the leaders at your church with the ways Christian faith can affect the ethical systems of the workplace?

- If you have the power of the pulpit, how could you use sermons and talks to illustrate ways that people have cultivated positive change in their organizational systems to better align their workplaces with kingdom values?

8

RESTRICTED ROLES FOR WOMEN

So God created mankind in his own image,
in the image of God he created them;
male and female he created them.

GENESIS 1:27

"WOMEN WERE DESIGNED by God to be good wives and mothers who maintain the house, cook the meals, and care for the children, while men were designed by God to be heads of households and responsible for financial provision for the family."[1] Those are the messages both of us received from our church communities growing up. And for both of us, education was highly valued—we got messages that we should pursue higher education and use our intellectual talent in school—yet in our churches we were not given positive models of how to use our education toward a career or how we might integrate our faith with our work.[2]

---

[1] Parts of this chapter and some of chapter nine are adapted from Oneya Fennell Okuwobi, Denise Daniels, and Elaine Howard Ecklund, "The Limits of Congregational Support for Working Women," *Review of Religious Research* 65, no. 3 (September 2023): 295-316.

[2] Such views were still alive and well at the time we wrote this book. See Bianca Brosh, "Chiefs Kicker Harrison Butker Wants Women to Be Homemakers. Does That Include His Physicist Mother?," MSNBC, May 16, 2024, www.msnbc.com/know-your-value/out-of-office/chiefs-harrison-butker-wants-women-homemakers-include-physicist-mother-rcna152626.

A number of years ago, Elaine decided she would visit a church to start building a community. When she asked the pastor about church programs and ministries she could join, he asked whether she was married and then whether her husband was attending church with her. Elaine told him she was recently married but living apart from her husband as they finished up academic work in different cities. It did not sound like the "young married" group would be a good fit because that was only for couples; the pastor implied that it was for couples who were living together. When he mentioned that some of the women in the church baked cookies for the children's Sunday school hour, Elaine explained that she was not much of a baker, so that probably was not the best fit either. "Well, other women bake muffins!" he replied.

Historically in the United States, churches have been set up around traditional gender roles, where men are primary breadwinners and women are primary family caregivers, and this pastor was trying to slot Elaine into a place in the church accordingly. He did not ask questions about her work or other interests to discern her true best fit for serving the church. Instead, he suggested work in the kitchen. In most of the churches Elaine and her husband have attended over the course of their life together, her husband, who actually *is* a very good baker, has never been asked to make cookies.

Denise has had similar experiences. When she and her husband had three young children, they started attending a new church, and she was asked whether she would be willing to work in the nursery or teach children's Sunday school classes; the implication was that only these two roles would be the right fit. Even though both Denise and her husband were professionals and both worked for pay outside the home, her husband was not asked whether he would like to take care of or teach children at church, and she was not asked whether she was interested in serving in any ministries that did not involve children. They eventually both volunteered in the nursery and preschool classes, and then taught second- and third-grade Sunday school together for almost a decade, but her husband was always a bit of an anomaly as a man teaching young kids, and Denise wondered whether her gifts should have been used in other ways in their church.

The view that men and women have different and distinct roles carries over into parachurch settings. For a number of years, Denise helped facilitate a monthly breakfast for Christian workplace professionals at her university. The breakfast was an opportunity to hear from an outside speaker and get to know other Christians in the marketplace. Likely because the event was held in the morning—a time that is particularly challenging for moms responsible for getting their children ready for daycare or school—most of the participants who came to the breakfast were men. One month, the speaker was the leader of a nationwide organization that developed and supported weekly small groups for Christian workplace leaders and was expanding into Denise's geographic region. It became very clear over the course of the speaker's talk that the groups were designed for men. When Denise asked him whether there were any groups that included women, he looked a little surprised and told her that there were not; thinking out loud, he suggested that it would be hard for men's groups to allow women to participate. Perhaps, he added, the organization would be willing to support women's groups if Denise were willing to start one. She did in fact become a member of the first women's group within this organization, but for many years it was the only one, and the women in the group often felt like outsiders. To this day, there are not mixed-gender groups within this organization.

These stories are from some time ago, and times have changed, as have some churches. Both our culture and our churches are more accepting than they used to be of women who work outside the home. But our research shows that these changes may not be as significant and pervasive as some might expect. Just this year Denise was part of a monthly faith-and-work gathering where she was often the only woman present. After several years of regular meetings, the group was ending, and a couple of options were presented to group members for alternative gatherings that they could attend instead. The alternatives were men-only groups.

Up to this point, we have looked at the ways Christians bring their faith to work and we have offered new ways they can do so that either advance or break old paradigms. Here we change the focus to examine the relationship between faith and work in the opposite direction—namely, how pastors and churches respond when women try to bring their work to church. We find that across all types of Christian churches and denominations, women who work are less supported in their professional endeavors than men. To understand why, we will start by considering how Christian women experience and express their faith at work, then look at the church itself as a workplace and examine the experiences of working women at church.

GENDERED EXPRESSION OF FAITH AT WORK

Women are generally more religious than men.[3] When we look at measures of religious commitment, we discover that women in the United States are more likely to pray daily, more likely to attend services weekly, and more likely to say religion is "very important" to them. In part because they are more likely than men to be religious, women may be primed to engage and express their faith at work. We found that women at all levels of the workplace hierarchy are more likely than men

---

[3]"The Gender Gap in Religion Around the World," Pew Research Center, March 22, 2016, www .pewforum.org/2016/03/22/the-gender-gap-in-religion-around-the-world/. See also the Faith at Work survey; Landon Schnabel, "The Gender Pray Gap: Wage Labor and the Religiosity of High-Earning Women and Men," *Gender & Society* 30, no. 4 (2016): 643-69; Marta Trzebia-towska and Steve Bruce, *Why Are Women More Religious Than Men?* (New York: Oxford University Press, 2012). There is some recent data showing that in the US men are for the first time surpassing women in church attendance, but this is a particularly interesting phenomenon because it is different from historical norms. It remains to be seen whether this will be a long-term pattern. For more information, see Daniel A. Cox and Kelsey Eyre Hammond, "Young Women Are Leaving Church in Unprecedented Numbers," American Enterprise Institute, April 4, 2024, www.aei.org/articles/young-women-are-leaving-church-in-unprecedented -numbers/.

to say they display or wear items that represent their faith or spirituality at work. We also found that women at all levels of their organizations agreed more than men that their faith or spirituality helps them experience meaning and purpose in their daily tasks. Women are also more likely than men to report praying or meditating at work, say they use their faith to act with integrity at work, and say that their faith helps them understand the ways the products or services produced by their organizations are meaningful.

On two items from our survey, however, men were significantly more likely than women to report their agreement. Men were more likely to say that they speak out against unfair work practices and that they are more motivated to talk about their faith or spirituality at work. We think this might be because men generally feel more empowered to speak up at work. The finding is also consistent with the view that the opportunity to enact religious identity is a strong predictor of whether a person does so. Given cultural gender norms, men may have more opportunity to enact their religious identity in a vocal way.[4] A wealth of research on gendered communication styles finds that women are frequently penalized for being direct and overt.[5] Our finding may also reflect a lack of confidence on the part of women in their ability to affect change or influence others' opinions, another finding that has been consistently supported by research.[6] It is also possible that faith at work functions differently for men than women because of their relative power in the workplace due to gender bias.

---

[4]See YingFei Héliot, Ilka H. Gleibs, Adrian Coyle, Denise M. Rousseau, and Céline Rojon, "Religious Identity in the Workplace: A Systematic Review, Research Agenda, and Practical Implications," *Human Resource Management* 59, no. 2 (2019): 153-73.

[5]See Alice H. Eagly and Linda L. Carli, *Through the Labyrinth: The Truth About How Women Become Leaders* (Cambridge, MA: Harvard Business School Press, 2007). See also Tracy Taylor, "Little Ladies Should Be Seen and Not Heard: A Study of Gender Bias in the Communication of Female Educational Leader" (PhD diss., Texas Tech University, 2012).

[6]See Tessie H. H. Herbst, "Gender Differences in Self-Perception Accuracy: The Confidence Gap and Women Leaders' Underrepresentation in Academia," *SA Journal of Industrial Psychology* 46, no. 1 (2020): 1-8. See also Katty Kay and Claire Shipman, *The Confidence Code: The Science and Art of Self-Assurance—What Women Should Know* (New York: Harper Business, 2020).

Perhaps men integrate faith in the workplace in ways that overtly reference and reinforce their power, while women do so more to cope with powerlessness and status frustrations at work. In other words, it may be that men experience and express religion more externally in the workplace, while women in the workplace engage their faith more internally.

Comparing Christian men and women in expression of faith at work

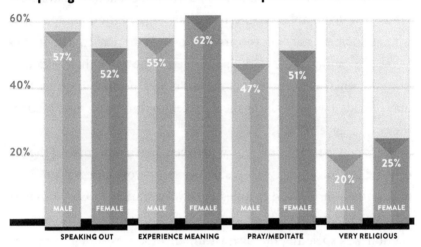

Percentages for are those that somewhat or strongly agree with the following statements:
- **Speak Out**—I express my view when I observe unfair work practices that conflict with my faith.
- **Experience Meaning**—My faith/spirituality helps me experience meaning and purpose in my daily work.
- **Pray/Meditate**—I benefit from praying or meditating privately at work.

Very Religious are those who indicate they are very religious, independently of religious service attendance.

Data: Faith at Work Main and Supplementary Surveys

Figure 8.1

Women in senior positions. While in general women are more likely than men to identify religion as an important aspect of their lives, there are some exceptions. Past research has found no significant differences in how religious *high-income* men and women are, which may explain why our research found that faith has less salience for women in senior positions in their organizations.[7] Women in leadership roles said they experienced more meaning in their work compared with those toward the bottom of their organization. But women at the top were significantly less likely than those in the middle of their organization to display or wear items that represented their faith or spirituality at work.[8] Women at the bottom or middle of their organization were more likely to say that they benefit from praying or meditating privately at work. We take from this that faith plays a different role for women at the top of an organization compared to women in other places in the organization. Faith may contribute to a sense of meaning in the work that women at the top of their organizations do, whereas for women at the bottom of the organizations, faith may provide a way of helping them to make it through in the situations they experience at work.

We found very few differences between men and women at the top of their organizations with respect to faith-work integration. Men and women in leadership roles look very similar to each other in terms of whether and how they engage faith at work. The one exception was speaking out against unfair practices—men at the top were significantly more likely than women at the top to report that they speak out against unfair practices at work. It could be that even women at the top feel less agency than their male counterparts. This is consistent with research on gender and leadership, which suggests that women are often socially sanctioned for direct and assertive speech and behavior.[9] That is, women at the top of their organizations may feel less able to say something about unfair practices at work because they perceive that their speaking out would not really

---

[7] Orestes P. Hastings and D. Michael Lindsay, "Rethinking Religious Gender Differences: The Case of Elite Women," *Sociology of Religion* 74, no. 4 (2013): 471-95; see also Schnabel, "Gender Pray Gap."

[8] This is compared to women in the middle of the leadership hierarchy of their organization.

[9] See in particular Anne M. Koenig, Alice H. Eagly, Abigail A. Mitchell, and Tiina Ristikari, "Are Leader Stereotypes Masculine? A Meta-analysis of Three Research Paradigms," *Psychological Bulletin* 137, no. 4 (2011): 616-42.

make a difference, or perhaps be personally detrimental, when compared to their male colleagues.

The uniqueness of evangelical Christian women. When we look at the experiences of women from different religious traditions (evangelical, mainline Protestant, Catholic, Muslim, Jewish, and none), we find that evangelical women report the lowest levels of sex-based discrimination at work. On its face, this seems a little odd. What is it about evangelical women that would lead them to experience less sex-based discrimination than women with other religious identities?

Men and women who report unfair treatment at work due to sex or gender by religious tradition

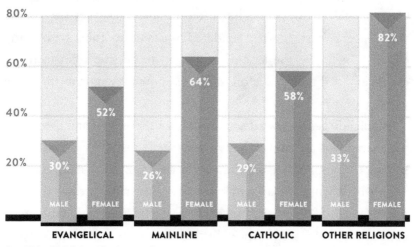

Data: Faith at Work Main and Supplementary Surveys

Figure 8.2

There are a several possibilities. It could be evangelical women select into or find themselves in organizations where there is less gender discrimination. But research also shows that women at the top of organizations are most likely to report experiences of gender discrimination or harassment in their careers, and evangelical Christian women are less likely than women from other religious groups to reach the highest levels of an organization. So perhaps because they are less likely to rise to the top of organizations, evangelical women may be less likely to experience those situations in which gender discrimination is most likely to occur. Finally, evangelical women may be less likely than other women to actually notice gender discrimination, possibly because they have been socialized through their churches to see different treatment of men and women as normal.

GENDERED WORK AT CHURCH

We turn now to an examination of the church and how churches may contribute in positive and negative ways to the experiences of Christian women who work. We argue that churches both create and perpetuate cultural understandings of gender that influence not only the experiences people have at church but also the experiences they have in the workplace. We start with gendered norms and roles within the church—including the lack of women in leadership roles in many churches—and then move on to discuss how these norms influence women at work.

People "do gender," what sociologists Candace West and Don Zimmerman define as "doing" the everyday "activities that cast particular pursuits as expressions of masculine and feminine 'natures.'"[10] In other words, while sex is based in biology, gender is expressed through one's behaviors. Whether those behaviors are perceived as more masculine or feminine is influenced by the culture. Organizations are part of the cultural landscape that communicates expected norms of behavior for men and women. Religious organizations, in particular, seem to create rules and communicate expectations that reinforce particular gender-role expectations and inequities as part of the spiritual order of things. For example, and perhaps somewhat surprising given mainline Protestant churches' gender-egalitarian stance, mainline Protestant mothers are less likely to work full time than

---

[10]See Candace West and Don H. Zimmerman, "Doing Gender," *Gender and Society* 1, no. 2 (1987): 125-51.

either evangelical Protestant or Catholic mothers when controlling for socioeconomic factors.[11]

These gender patterns within churches can be seen most particularly in pastoral and leadership roles.[12] While in many cases there are theological rationales for disparities between men and women in church leadership, this disparity somewhat surprisingly exists in both theologically conservative and liberal churches. In denominations and traditions that ordain women into pastor positions, women still face challenges related to their gender. Social work scholar Katie Lauve-Moon, for example, investigated the experiences of women clergy in a denomination that was founded expressly to support women's ministerial leadership.[13] She concluded that even in these churches, gender inequality is often embedded in "policies, culture, symbols and images, division of labor, interactions, organizational logic, bodies, and individual internalizations, in ways that are mutually reinforcing and most often negatively affect women professionals and leaders."[14] As a result, even in the context of a progressive denomination, women are underrepresented in pastoral leadership positions.

That Christian clergy remain overwhelmingly male can create difficulties for women in the church, whether they are church leaders or congregants.[15] Yet, it is possible and indeed common for men to act as mentors and provide spiritual direction for women in the church. An additional problem arises when male pastoral leaders *choose* not to

---

[11]See, for example, W. Bradford Wilcox, "Religion, Convention, and Paternal Involvement," *Journal of Marriage and Family* 64, no. 3 (2002): 780-92.

[12]See Joan Acker, "Inequality Regimes: Gender, Class, and Race in Organizations," *Gender & Society* 20, no. 4 (2006): 441-64. See also Samantha K. Ammons and Penny Edgell, "Religious Influences on Work-Family Trade-Offs," *Journal of Family Issues* 28, no. 6 (2007): 794-826; Andrew L. Whitehead, "Gendered Organizations and Inequality Regimes: Gender, Homosexuality, and Inequality Within Religious Congregations," *Journal for the Scientific Study of Religion* 52, no. 3 (2013): 476-93.

[13]Katie Lauve-Moon, *Preacher Woman: A Critical Look at Sexism Without Sexists* (New York: Oxford University Press, 2021), 187.

[14]See the conclusion in Lauve-Moon, *Preacher Woman.*

[15]Cyrus Schleifer and Amy D. Miller, "Occupational Gender Inequality Among American Clergy, 1976–2016: Revisiting the Stained-Glass Ceiling," *Sociology of Religion* 78, no. 4 (2018): 387-410.

provide support for women. More often than not, the male clergy we interviewed chose not to provide the same support for working women that they do for working men. We did not see the same unidirectional support for one gender over another among the female clergy we interviewed. In a sense, then, the deficit in support for women who work that we find in the church is partially the result of a lack of support for women in the clergy.

Across all church types, we heard from women congregants and pastors who confirmed that churches support male and female workers differently. Our interview respondents pointed to pastors' lack of engagement with women generally, inattention to issues affecting women specifically, and demands that churches place on women's time, all of which send implicit messages degrading the value of women's work. "I think that how society or organizations or institutions approach men and women is always different. So, I would say that the church is no different than that, that they always look at men and women differently, on their roles in the church, on the kind of support that they need, how they view their contribution to society, and the expectation of what they're supposed to do," said a mainline Protestant woman who could not put her finger on what was different in the treatment of men and women in her church but compared it to the disparate treatment she experienced in other organizations.[16] "So, I think, therefore, it will always be that way," she said in a spirit of defeat.

Communicating traditional gender roles. While all Christian denominations are alike in their implicit lack of support for women who work, in a few evangelical and Black Protestant churches we found even more explicit messages deterring women from working. These messages can make women who work feel ostracized, or at best anomalous. Evangelical churches are especially likely to promote gender essentialism as central to the church and society, creating rigid gender

---

[16]F@W_ST113, White woman, age 62, sales, mainline, interview conducted August 13, 2019.

hierarchies that pervade multiple aspects of life, including work.[17] An evangelical nurse, for example, told us, "I have been to one faith community [where] women are not necessarily encouraged to work outside the home, and there is some condemnation, which I feel is wrong."[18] A physician who attends an evangelical church, Rochelle, told us how difficult it is to ignore some of the Christian messages about women working outside the home.[19] "If you're raised [to believe] that women are supposed to be in the home and this, that, and the other, then you find that you're really not meant to be at home, I think it's much more challenging," she said. As she asserts, messages delivered through church and home as a child are difficult to escape and often become influential during one's own family formation.

Gendered expectations can also be pronounced within Black Protestant churches, but for different reasons. Our respondents told us that conservative Black Protestant churches have traditionally been places where male leadership is affirmed, in part, because of the difficulties Black men face in other areas of society. Ironically, structural impediments to the financial achievement of Black men, such as discrimination, have always left Black women more likely to need to work, regardless of religious beliefs.[20] A Black financial analyst attending a mainline Black Protestant church told us about the resistance she sensed when bringing her work experience to bear on her church's finance committee.[21] "There was a man who was a manager at a fast-food store. And so he would get up and tell you about how he did this at Burger King or whatever. [But] when I got up and said something

---

[17]Patricia Homan and Amy Burdette, "When Religion Hurts: Structural Sexism and Health in Religious Congregations," *American Sociological Review* 86, no. 2 (2021): 234-55.

[18]F@W ST98, Black woman, age 60, registered nurse, evangelical, interview conducted July 10, 2019.

[19]F@W_ST137, Black woman, age 43, physician, evangelical, interview conducted September 23, 2019.

[20]Jennifer Glass and Leda E. Nath, "Religious Conservatism and Women's Market Behavior Following Marriage and Childbirth," *Journal of Marriage and Family* 68, no. 3 (2006): 611-29.

[21]F@W_ST18, Black woman, age 45, financial analyst, Black Protestant, interview conducted November 28, 2018.

because I actually do work at a bank, they were like, 'Well, you think you know something,'" she told us. She said her experience was vocally dismissed even though it was more relevant to the issue at hand than that of her fellow congregant who is a man. This incident matches a framework she has heard in her church before. "Every once in a while, you'll hear somebody say the problems in the Black community are caused because women are tryin' to be men," she said.

A pastor echoed this sentiment by valorizing the work of men as central to their identities and blaming society for what he sees as confusion in gender roles.[22] "I don't know that people have the same regard for gender roles that perhaps we once had. You know, the Bible is pretty strong on there being roles for different genders. And we have to preach the Bible, right? So. But I don't think society has maintained regards to those roles," he said. As a result, this pastor believes that men feel less appreciated because they have been pushed out of their role as breadwinner for their families. "Men say, I love you because I bring bacon. You have bacon so you should know I love you, right? But, you know, now we get bacon from so many different places," he explained. This language would seem to devalue women who bring home the bacon themselves, as well as men who seek a role apart from or beyond that of financial provider.[23]

Being above reproach. In 1 Timothy, the apostle Paul writes, "Therefore an overseer must be above reproach, the husband of one wife, sober-minded, self-controlled, respectable, hospitable, able to teach, not a drunkard, not violent but gentle, not quarrelsome, not a lover of money" (1 Timothy 3:2-3 ESV). Over time, this verse has been used to justify male pastors not meeting alone with women in order to be above reproach, avoiding even the appearance of any impropriety.

---

[22]F@W_PA01, Black man, age 53, pastor, Black Protestant, interview conducted April 10, 2019.

[23]We want to stress that there is a literature that shows exception to what our respondents said about the roles of men and women in largely Black churches; see, for example, Yolanda Pierce, 2023. *In my Grandmother's House: Black Women, Faith, and the Stories We Inherit* (Minneapolis: Broadleaf Books, 2023).

Noted evangelist Billy Graham was famous for not traveling, meeting, or eating alone with a woman other than his wife, leading to what is now known among evangelicals as the Billy Graham rule. He famously sent his male advisers ahead of him to make sure there were no women lurking in his hotel room. (Of course, this rule, which reflects concerns about the potential complications that might arise when women and men interact, ignores the possibility of problematic interactions with those of one's own gender.)

In a similar fashion, one-third of pastors we spoke to said they do not feel comfortable talking to women about their jobs in a one-on-one setting. This refusal to talk with women alone has discipleship consequences for women and the broader church environment. One evangelical pastor said he probably tends to talk more about work with men than women "just because I think I feel a little more comfort in doing that maybe as a pastor, like male to male versus male to female, though I do have conversations and meetings with females as well. But most of it is, I think, male to male because maybe men feel that I can relate to them better."[24] This pastor almost seemed taken aback by his own comment, then reflected on why he provides different levels of support by gender. "I think it just maybe has to do with being a pastor and not wanting to be in a position of [meeting with people] across genders, you know, being above reproach," he said, referencing the biblical command in the epistle to Timothy.

Other pastors shared this preference for providing support to men over women, often not recognizing how this could exclude women from important conversations. One pastor who leads an interdenominational church said that because he has a legal background, he often provides his parishioners with informal legal support, especially when it comes to incidents that potentially involve racial or religious discrimination, but his expertise is not offered equally to men and women

---

[24]F@W_PA09, White man, age 52, pastor, evangelical, interview conducted March 9, 2020.

in the congregation.[25] He said that in general he prefers not to talk alone to congregants who are women. He told us that his wife, who also works at the church, can fulfill that task—even though she does not have expertise related to work and discrimination claims. "There are occasions when I may talk to a woman, but [my wife is] there, and I really don't have to do that," he said.

This pastor's preference for meeting with men one-on-one is also reflected in his response to our question of whether he feels he understands the lives of people at work. "I think I have a pretty good understanding about them [working people] because we do talk, like we have a breakfast for men once a month. Men share what they are going through, their pressures, their goals, their concerns, and even how that work situation may be putting a conflict at home [laughs]," he said, referring exclusively to his interactions with men in the church. This pastor believes he has a good understanding of the issues faced by his congregants who work while regularly interacting with less than half the congregation on these issues.

Clergy wives. The wives of clergymen often make possible their husband's relative isolation from women congregants. Although pastors' wives are not typically official church employees, congregants regularly assume that they will take on major church responsibilities. One Christian woman we interviewed, who works as an engineer, described her church to us by saying: "They have a huge staff, and even though all the pastors are male, their wives have a huge part in [pastoring]. A pastor's wife can be a huge support for the women of the church, in ways that her husband can't really talk to certain subjects, I guess."[26]

Meanwhile, pastors who are women regularly minister to men, and we did not hear refusals from them about meeting alone with male congregants. A Catholic pastoral associate told us she felt that her effectiveness depended on being able to minister to women and men

---

[25]F@W_PA02, Black man, age 67, pastor, Black Protestant, interview conducted April 10, 2019.
[26]F@W_ST39, White woman, 39, engineer, evangelical, interview conducted January 16, 2019.

alike so that she would not be limited in her role.[27] "I'm just working like everybody else," she said, "and so I don't think about them being male or female, you know?" Although clergymen can decide not to talk one-on-one with someone of the opposite sex, claiming it is for the protection of their reputation, clergywomen are not afforded that luxury. They are expected to meet one-on-one with men in their congregations as part of their leadership position. None of the married women pastors we interviewed talked about having their husbands meet with men in the church.

Women's stories of work marginalized. Across our conversations with parishioners and pastors, we found that women's stories of work life were not seen as mainstream and remained untold in spaces such as Sunday morning gatherings, where both men and women attended. This was not due to simple ignorance; nearly every pastor we interviewed named challenges faced by women who work, including gender discrimination, sexual harassment, and tensions between work and family. Less than one-third of women congregants we interviewed, however, said they had heard a sermon or pastoral message that mentioned women's work concerns, though most had heard their pastors discuss men's work concerns. The deficit meant that women recognized they were not receiving training and encouragement in church for their work lives. "It isn't like I sit in the pew on Sunday and get a lecture about how women should be home raising families. . . . But I think many Catholic women are working women with families, and I'm not sure there's much of a nod to that ever," lamented one Catholic woman who works as a professor.[28] This not only leaves women's concerns illaddressed but also deprives male congregants from learning about the experiences of working women and seeing the treatment of women in

---

[27] F@W_PA03, Hispanic woman, age 65, pastoral associate, Catholic, interview conducted April 12, 2019.
[28] F@W_ST36, White woman, age 45, associate professor, Catholic, interview conducted January 10, 2019.

the workplace as an issue to which they are able to bring Christian moral reflection.

In large part, this deficit comes from the belief that a woman's primary work is in the home. "There's the traditional idea that you're in the home, and if you're away from the home, it's just to reinforce the home," said a Catholic film director who feels marginalized both for being a Latina and for being a Christian.[29] Echoing Denise's experiences discussed at the beginning of this chapter, the film director mentioned, "[In most churches] there are no women professional groups, but they do often [have ones for men]. . . . It's weird." She told us that the women's groups at her church tend to be invested in skills such as knitting, which are not of use to her in the professional world. A nurse who considers herself an evangelical Christian said there is different support in her church for working men from working women, and in one church she attended, criticism was expressed toward women who worked outside the home.[30] While she respects women who stay home with their children, "We shouldn't be putting each other down for the choices that we make to care for our families," she said.

The Christian women we talked with also felt that issues uniquely affecting women in the workplace were not given the same emphasis as other social issues. A college recruiter in a mainline church spoke with us about being dismissed at work because of her gender.[31] "I bring a lot to the table," she said. "Unfortunately, sometimes I just gotta bring my own chair!" While she has had small-group discussions with other women congregants about workplace issues facing women, including sexual harassment, she has never heard any of these issues addressed from the pulpit. "That conversation tends to occur more individually as opposed to from a pulpit," she told us. "I would love to hear somebody from a

---

[29]F@W_SUP16, Hispanic woman, age 34, film director, Catholic, interview conducted December 6, 2021.

[30]F@W_ST98, White woman, age 60, registered nurse, evangelical, interview conducted July 10, 2019.

[31]F@W_ST97, White woman, age 39, college recruiter, mainline, interview conducted July 9, 2019.

pulpit say something like that." By comparison, "I think racism has been covered," she said. "My pastor has been very quick to say about racism that 'biblically, this is wrong. This is not just a moral issue, but as Christians and as believers, you speak out against this because this is wrong.'" While she agrees with the emphasis on racism, it makes her think, "I don't know why this hasn't been discussed in regard to the #MeToo movement." Even in a mainline church willing to tackle social issues in a public forum, topics concerning women were seen as the province of women's groups rather than a call to action for the church as a whole.

Scheduling assumes women do not work. Working Christian women often told us that their church communities can be insensitive to women's schedules, particularly professional demands, which is not the case with men. Those we interviewed said that women's church activities are more likely to be scheduled during the workday, while activities targeted at men tend to be scheduled outside typical working hours. This scheduling can limit the ability of women who work to participate in activities supposedly designed for them. The Catholic professor we introduced earlier in this chapter told us how the timing of events at her church devalues women's work.[32] "Opportunities for women to become involved in parish life, like through a women's group or different committees, the times at which those things meet do not work with a working woman's schedule," she said. "They'll have meetings at 10 a.m. on a Wednesday morning or 1 p.m. on Thursday afternoon. So, it's there very implicitly as opposed to explicitly, whereas most of the stuff that's gauged on trying to get men involved in different things, those activities are at night or on Saturdays." A lawyer who attends a mainline church was frustrated that the most-attended activity for women at her church is a moms' group that meets during working hours.[33] She asked her leadership, "What we can do to foster those

---

[32]F@W_ST36, White woman, age 45, associate professor, Catholic, interview conducted January 10, 2019.
[33]F@W_ST141, White woman, age 39, lawyer, mainline, interview conducted October 3, 2019.

relationships for people that can't make a 9:30 a.m. on Friday meeting?" No solutions have been suggested.

Like Denise's and Elaine's experiences, the kinds of volunteer activities women are asked to engage in are gendered, usually involving care work. The lawyer mentioned above described how women are often asked to perform volunteer labor instead of men. "The children's ministry always asks the mothers to work," she said. "One time I was walking out of my class, and the director was looking for a teacher for the next week. She walked past my husband and my friend's husband and went to my friend and asked her. And I'm like, 'You just passed two people.'" Christian women assumed they would provide more volunteer time and effort than men to keep the church functioning.[34] They recognize that they are disproportionately called on to volunteer. Another woman described how churches would not be sustainable without women's efforts.[35] As she put it, "Women are just culturally the caregivers. They are the ones that nurture these important institutions. They do all the behind-the-scenes work that men do not usually do. And they see the value in creating nurturing organizations, such as church families. Men just benefit from it [laughs]."

A woman who works as a salesperson sensed that assumptions about men's work responsibilities led to women becoming overwhelmed with volunteer duties, even when they also are working.[36] "I honestly think there's an underlying feeling that the men work harder," she said. "You know, that there's a little more understanding for them," that because they work harder they cannot do as much church volunteering. As a result, this woman took on volunteer tasks at her church even when she was already overloaded. "Sometimes I'm telling them verbally, I'm

---

[34]See Chao Guo, Natalie J. Webb, Rikki Abzug, and Laura R. Peck, "Religious Affiliation, Religious Attendance, and Participation in Social Change Organizations," *Nonprofit and Voluntary Sector Quarterly* 42, no. 1 (2013): 34-58.

[35]F@W_SUP21, Hispanic woman, age 54, director of program management, mainline, interview conducted December 17, 2021.

[36]F@W_ST161, Hispanic woman, age 51, educator, mainline, interview conducted November 20, 2019.

tired, don't ask me to do one more thing 'cause I'm tired," she told us, "but the men they don't ask to do as much because, well, they're working." Women also sensed that it was unacceptable for them to miss church activities due to work obligations, though that was not the case for men. "Men aren't asked as often to teach Sunday school or to . . . take care of the little kids and volunteer in the nursery. And if, oh, God forbid, a woman has to work and misses Bible study, but a man, that's expected," said a realtor we spoke with, discussing how her Southern Baptist church was quicker to dismiss her work responsibilities if they got in the way of volunteering.[37] A teacher told us that she felt judged if work commitments interfered with church, also feeling that her paid work was not valued.[38] As she explained,

> At a parish council meeting, if one of the male members of the parish council says, "Oh, I have a work thing, I can't meet then," everybody just says, of course, uh-huh. But if a woman says, "Oh, I have a work thing, I can't meet then," . . . there's just this little bit of a judgy atmosphere, like you're not managing your time well or your priorities aren't straight, or do you really have something important at work, how important is that?

In her view, "I think we are still struggling with some deeply ingrained sexism that says that men's work is more important."

It surprised us that in both traditional and more progressive congregations there are similar mechanisms disadvantaging women who work. This is not to say that there are no theological differences between those congregations but, despite that, there are some surprising similarities in their lack of support for women's paid labor. Pastors, both male and female, feel the need to effectively minister to men who work in particular. Men are seen as the prototypical worker, and knowing and responding to their work-related issues and concerns is seen as enough. Women tend to be seen as caregivers and church volunteers—even

---

[37]F@W_ST130, White woman, age 44, realtor, evangelical, interview conducted September 11, 2019.
[38]F@W_ST103, White woman, age 57, librarian, mainline, interview conducted July 18, 2019.

though many women see being a worker as one of their central identities. Previous research has speculated that elite women tend to be less
religious because high-achieving men receive validation in religious
communities, but similarly positioned women do not.[39] Our research
uncovered numerous examples of congregations and their leaders
failing to support and sometimes even hindering women's workforce
participation by neglecting to provide pastoral support for women, not
treating working women's concerns as mainstream, or not considering
women's work schedules. The messages received about work within the
church were nearly always targeted toward men and left women with
the impression that their work is perceived as less valuable.

This leaves a significant gap for women looking to integrate their
work and faith. Women in these churches are offered a faith identity
without a significant place for their professional lives, potentially exac-
erbating gender inequality. In the next chapter, we discuss the ways that
some churches and church leaders *are* supporting women in the workplace and other ways that they could do so even better. We will also
discuss what Christian leaders and workers in a variety of occupations
might do to better support men and women flourishing at work.

REFLECTION QUESTIONS

For everyone

- What implicit or overt messages have you heard about the appropriate roles for men and women in the workplace?
- What implicit or overt messages have you heard about the appropriate roles for men and women in the home?
- What implicit or overt messages have you heard about the appropriate roles for men and women in the church?
- Where do these messages come from? Do you agree with them?

---

[39]See Landon Schnabel, "Religion and Gender Equality Worldwide: A Country-Level Analysis,"
Social Indicators Research 129, no. 2 (2016): 893-907.

For faith communities

- To what extent does your church equally encourage women and men to use their talents and giftings in the workplace, home, and church?
- To what extent does your congregation support men and women who work outside the home?
- How could your congregation make changes that empower women at work, and how might you influence those changes?

9

MEN AND WOMEN FLOURISHING TOGETHER

When Esther's words were reported to Mordecai, he sent back this answer: "Do not think that because you are in the king's house you alone of all the Jews will escape. For if you remain silent at this time, relief and deliverance for the Jews will arise from another place, but you and your father's family will perish. And who knows but that you have come to your royal position for such a time as this?"

ESTHER 4:12-14

THE FIRST CHAPTERS of Esther seem to suggest that Esther was chosen to be queen because she won a beauty pageant held by the king.[1] But as the story progresses it becomes clear that Esther was a leader. She was a strategic risk-taker. In the Persian court in that era, the consequence of approaching the throne room without a summons from the king was death unless the king intervened. Yet, knowing this, Esther still chose to approach the king to save the Jewish people from a pogrom. She was savvy and shrewd while at the same time other-focused.

---

[1]See Warren Wiersbe, *Life Sentences: Discover the Themes of 63 Bible Characters* (Grand Rapids, MI: Zondervan, 2007).

The model of Esther is found in spirit in the New Testament as well. Beth Allison Barr writes in her bestseller *The Making of Biblical Womanhood,*

> In a world that didn't accept the word of a woman as a valid witness, Jesus chose women as witnesses for his resurrection. In a world that gave husbands power over the very lives of their wives, the apostle Paul told husbands to do the opposite—to give up their lives for their wives. In a world that saw women as biologically deformed men, monstrous even, Paul declared that men were just like women in Christ.

In the time of Esther and in many times and places since, women could not own property, did not have legal rights to their children, and were often viewed as expendable. In many ways, women have made great strides in gender equality and their status in society. But as we saw in the last chapter, women still struggle to achieve role equality in family, church, and work. Christian women have often been ascribed roles by the church that focus on private home life rather than the public workplace.[2] Even for women who have power in their organizations, there are still societal expectations that diminish the potential for women's flourishing and that women must counteract. For example, research that examines how leaders write letters of recommendation show that they tend to describe women, even women in top leadership positions, as embodying characteristics that are likely to be seen as weaker, using what researchers call "grindstone" words, including phrases such as "hardworking" and "gets tasks done" rather than standout words and phrases such as "leader" and "pathbreaking work."[3] Positive portrayals of women at work include descriptions of them as good followers, nice, kind, easy to get along with, and compliant, characteristics that are not generally associated with men or with leaders

---

[2]Beth Allison Barr, *The Making of Biblical Womanhood: How the Subjugation of Women Became Gospel Truth* (Grand Rapids, MI: Brazos, 2021).
[3]There is other research on this topic, but see for example Kuheli Dutt, Danielle L. Pfaff, Ariel F. Bernstein, Joseph S. Dillard, and Caryn J. Block, "Gender Differences in Recommendation Letters for Postdoctoral Fellowships in Geoscience," *Nature Geosciences* 9 (2016): 805-8.

more broadly. Recommenders are more likely to describe men as having positions of strength, taking charge, able to get things done, and able to make hard decisions. In effect, they describe men as stronger and women as weaker, even though very little about most leadership has to do with physical strength. Research suggests that both male and female managers are less likely to give women high-risk tasks that may lead to future management roles.[4]

In the last chapter we saw how churches can contribute to and perpetuate some of these gender inequities that persist in our culture. In this chapter we examine some ways that churches and Christian workplace leaders can address such inequities and support women's flourishing in the workplace.[5] For example, some of those we interviewed said their churches go above and beyond in offering resources, services, and job support for everyone, which includes women. An evangelical land surveyor explained that there is no real difference in how his church supports women when compared to men.[6] He mentions as an example that

> If they lost their job or were searching for a job and needed help, you know, our church does get involved with that occasionally and say, "Look, so-and-so needs a job, or so-and-so lost their job, and we're going to support them for a while." I would say we probably help more women just based on who I've seen, but I don't think that's a choice; I think it's just how it's worked out.

The kind of help his congregation and congregations like this provide seems admirable. Christians especially should be concerned with justice and opportunity for all who are made in the image of God. Yet,

---

[4]Jenny M. Hoobler, Sandy J. Wayne, and Grace Lemmon, "Bosses' Perceptions of Family-Work Conflict and Women's Promotability: Glass Ceiling Effects," *Academy of Management Journal* 52, no. 5 (2009): 939-57.

[5]We draw on the examples from our own research for the suggestions in the remainder of this chapter. For readers interested in a fuller treatment of this topic, another excellent resource that provides more theological framing for why and how men and women should work together in the church is Rob Dixon, *Together in Ministry: Women and Men in Flourishing Partnerships* (Downers Grove, IL: InterVarsity Press, 2021).

[6]F@W_ST24, White man, age 31, land surveyor, evangelical, interview conducted December 6, 2018.

it is not always clear whether these respondents think women are disadvantaged in the working world. It seems that they minimize the importance of talking about gender equality. It is also not clear whether many congregations consider how women's needs and likelihood of facing discrimination at work might be different from men's. We argue that churches need to be more overt in their support of working women in particular, recognizing the unique challenges they face in the workplace and the unique demands they experience trying to maintain work-life balance.

Here, through the eyes of those we interviewed, we show how Christians might champion women's equality in workplaces. Based on our own experiences and those of other scholars and public thinkers, we offer ways that both congregations and workplaces might change. Here we will draw on our data to amplify what those we interviewed for our studies of faith at work say their congregations are doing well. We will hold these as models for what could be done by churches broadly. We also want to give advice to those in the workplace—both men and women—about how they can speak for and sponsor women's careers. We end by examining the importance of engaging in healthy patterns of work and rest as one means of supporting women who work.

While a sea change has not happened yet, we are seeing pockets of change and improvement—bright spots where churches or church leaders are better supporting women who work. And, as we will show, there are things that workplace Christians at every level can do to bring us toward greater gender equality.

WHAT SOME CHURCHES ARE DOING RIGHT

As we saw in the last chapter, support of working women begins in part with women being allowed to contribute their gifts more fully within the church. We recognize that there are real theological differences between various Christian traditions with respect to the particular roles that women might have freedom to take on in their churches, and yet these theological positions should not prevent women from serving and leading in the workplace.

Support women's giftings in the church. All congregations should engage with questions of how women's gifts in leadership, organization, communication, and decision making can be affirmed and utilized within churches. Congregations sometimes make a special point of sponsoring women leading. "We have women who go up there [to the pulpit] and speak, and we have one woman who is higher up in the leadership of the church, and when she's not doing that, she stocks shelves at a grocery store," said an evangelical man who works as an ROTC instructor as evidence of how his congregation approaches gender equity.[7]

> So, [our church leaders] show that anybody can be in a leadership position in the church, and that the fact that they let a woman speak or deliver a message one week, or have equal say-so as the men in the leadership, I think that promotes a balanced and equitable viewpoint on the role of women in the workplace, the role of men in the workplace, and—and ministering to them appropriately.

This man thinks that gender equality in his church is a sign of the church's overall attitude toward gender and work, and that what was demonstrated in the church was evidence of the ways that churches were likely to support men and women in the workplace. His excerpt also demonstrates the very real need to see and understand women as organizational leaders and as contributors, not just helpers.

A similar response was given by a woman who works as a Spanish teacher, who mentioned the roles of women in the church as evidence of support for women who work.[8] "They are very supportive of women who work," she said. "The pastor's wife works. The church treasurer is a woman. The person who does the organ is a woman. Are they supportive of women in the workplace? Yeah." Having women serve in church

---

[7]F@W_ST37, White/Hispanic man, age 43, high school ROTC instructor, evangelical, interview conducted January 10, 2019.

[8]F@W_ST19, White woman, age 55, Spanish teacher, evangelical, interview conducted November 28, 2018.

leadership roles and providing positive models of working women are ways that these churches signal support for women who work.

Talk about challenges working women experience. Our research reveals that some congregational leaders do recognize that most women now work for pay outside the home and that many women have experienced unequal workplace treatment. For example, a woman who works as a senior program manager at an education resources company said her pastor tries hard to acknowledge the kinds of challenges that women often face in workplaces.[9] She said,

> He is very attuned . . . very aware of the contributions of women and how they're not as respected as they should be and very aware of the inconsistencies in justice and treatment. And he pulls it into [his sermons] as he's talking about Bible stories and how Jesus treated women. And it's just very connected in with [the idea that] women were leaders in the church, in the early days, and we need to be aware of that.

Addressing women's inequality in the workplace, she explained, is part of her church's broader emphasis on the importance of diversity and equality in churches and workplaces. A man who works in politics seemed to also see his church's discussion of gender equality as a part of its broader emphasis on justice.[10] Gender "has definitely been brought up [at church] for equity and representation . . . in leadership, corporate boardrooms. . . . It has been brought up, specifically for equal pay," he said. "Every service will always have a male and a female pastor, [and] that is I think very groundbreaking, and it's kind of very progressive compared to the way other churches are structured."

A man who works as a nurse said that even though his pastor doesn't want to get "too controversial," he does try hard to point out the portions of biblical passages that clearly see women equally.[11] In particular,

---

[9]F@W_ST113, Hispanic woman, age 51, senior program manager at education resources company, mainline, interview conducted August 13, 2019.
[10]F@W_ST13, Filipino man, age 32, senior district representative, evangelical, conducted November 15, 2018.
[11]F@W_ST32, White man, age 38, nurse, Catholic, interview conducted December 19, 2018.

when discussing a controversial Bible passage that is used to support women's inequality, he "did try to cut short this idea that a woman should be [laughs], you know, at home, pregnant . . . when that actually isn't what the passage was really about originally; it's not even an interpretation. . . . [The pastor] does point out that . . . women should be allowed to be free to fulfill their life."

A woman who works as a manager in community engagement for a nonprofit told us her pastor talks about

> gender equality generally but not specifically in the workplace. But he does talk about gender equality in general. . . . He draws on his personal experiences. . . . I mean, it comes down to God loves all people. I mean, if we really just listen to the Bible about that. . . . But he just talks about how his life would never have been the same if everyone he interacted with looked the same as he did. And the pastor just really tries to break those color lines and the gender lines too. . . . So he talks about it from a biblical standpoint and then he also talks about it drawing on personal experiences.[12]

Although rare, there were respondents who specifically mentioned their pastors and church leaders addressing some of the subtexts about men's and women's work, such as the idea that husbands need to make more than their wives or that men and women are naturally suited for different kinds of jobs. A salesman who attends an evangelical church says he has heard empowering messages from his pastor's sermons: "The message was that men . . . don't have to make more than women, and he used the wage gap as an example. I don't remember the statement verbatim, but that was one of his main points was about men not needing to make more than women."[13] A Catholic woman talked about her priest, who had worked as a nurse by trade, sharing from the pulpit about the importance of gender equality at work.[14] She told us, "He has

---

[12]F@W_ST15, White woman, age 47, manager of community engagement, evangelical, interview conducted November 20, 2018.

[13]F@W_ST84, White man, age 21, salesman, evangelical, interview conducted June 12, 2019.

[14]F@W_ST69, Hispanic woman, age 40, administrative assistant, Catholic, interview conducted May 22, 2019.

very strong feelings that women should be able to do what men do, and men should be able to do what women do. So yeah. It is talked about quite a bit, normally."

Acknowledge workplace harassment. One of the particular challenges that working women face is sexual harassment and discrimination. While men can also be harassed and discriminated against because of their sex, it is far more common for women to have such experiences. Christian churches are still struggling with how to approach these issues. Several people we interviewed, however, shared with us ways that church leaders understand the possibility of gender-based harassment and discrimination at work and approach it through a scriptural or theological lens, addressing the issue in a way that supports those who have been targeted. A woman in her late twenties who works as a warehouse packer said her pastors "always tell us that we should never be discriminated [against] at work, especially in the United States. We should never be discriminated against because we are women or because we are Latinos, nobody should discriminate [against] us for that."

Church leaders also occasionally brought up #MeToo, the "social movement and awareness campaign against sexual abuse, sexual harassment, and rape culture," but when it was addressed, those we interviewed told us such mentions were most often focused on ways that men should behave at work rather than how those who were victimized might find support.[15] A man who works in human resources told us that after the #MeToo movement his pastor responded by "making sure that he is saying to the men like, 'Hey, you know, it's very important for you all to conduct yourselves as respectfully at all times.'"[16] A man who works as an engineer has been impressed by, in light of the current discussion of sexual harassment in workplaces, the way his pastor talks

---

[15]See "#MeToo Movement," Wikipedia, accessed December 5, 2024, https://en.wikipedia.org/wiki/MeToo_movement.

[16]F@WST73, Black man, age 31, human resources, evangelical, interview conducted May 29, 2019.

about current events: "When there was, you know, a lot of things going on with, you know, the MeToo movement . . . [he talked about] bringing the respect that everyone deserves not just to the workplace but your entire life."[17]

One woman who is a retired real estate agent, when asked whether her congregation's leaders ever bring up sexual harassment or #MeToo, told us: "It is something they have talked about in the sermon. Maybe an example when something like this happens, what to do, or how to handle it. And if you're the victim, or if you're the aggressor. I mean, no one's exempt." It is noteworthy that she mentions that her pastor has addressed how to handle being either the victim or the aggressor (hopefully in a way that challenges the aggressor to take responsibility and realize the effect of their actions). It was very rare for our respondents to say their pastors mention both sides like this or directly addressed the additional support women might need if they had been victimized in this way.

Create programming to support working women. There were a few congregations in which working women felt supported in both their family and workplace roles. In one of a very few examples, a communications specialist in a mainline church praised her congregation for the professional camaraderie that existed there.[18] She told the story of a friend of hers who was invited to a women's small group in the church. "She walked in, and one of [the other women] said, 'Are you a nerd like us?' It turns out she had gone to the one small group that was all working moms in tech. She ended up feeling like she was in a place where she really belonged in a group of people." She said her church is also intentional in providing support for working parents on the weekend rather than during the week. "We have a Parents' Day Out, so parents who work can bring their kids on Saturday morning. We do it

---

[17]F@W_ST72, White man, age 23, engineer, Catholic, interview conducted May 29, 2019.
[18]F@W_ST107, White woman, age 49, communication specialist, mainline, interview conducted August 1, 2019.

once a month and get like four or five hours of the day just to take care of them. Some of them do adult things without a kid following them around."

The conscious effort to create groups with like-minded women and the provision of support at times when working women can access it left this congregant feeling like she was well taken care of in her church community. This account also underscores how churches can make a large difference in how supported working women in the congregation feel by making relatively minor adjustments, such as being mindful in scheduling the timing of events. In contrast, we had many women respondents tell us that they could not attend women's events at church because they were scheduled during working hours. By recognizing the roles and needs of women explicitly, churches can support women in achieving success at work and balance in life.

So far, we have looked to identify the positive ways that churches engage with the unique experiences of gender, and how they can provide meaningful support to working women especially. But churches are somewhat limited in their ability to directly advance workplace cultures that promote justice. They work through their congregants. Much of the work that needs to be done must be done by those in the church who are engaging these workplace cultures and systems on a daily basis. That is, those who are in the workplace, and especially those who have power by virtue of their organizational roles, have a particular responsibility to attend to the needs of others.

WHAT WORKPLACE LEADERS CAN DO BETTER

Look for role models and become mentors. On the one hand, women need role models who show them that success in the workplace is possible and needed. Role models will not necessarily be those we know personally but can include anyone who has gone before us who shows us that success is possible. It is helpful for role models to be people who are like us in some appreciable ways; the extent to which we share characteristics with a role model improves our ability to relate to them and strengthens our belief in our own abilities. I may not know Beyonce, for example, but if I am a Black woman and want a musical career, seeing someone like her can give a kind of inspiration.

Mentors, on the other hand, are those we know and are in relationship with. We find a basis for mentorship in Christianity—Jesus' twelve disciples were in a sense those he knew intimately and those he mentored. We draw from education scholars Eugene Anderson and Anne Lucasse Shannon's definition of mentoring as a "nurturing process in which a more skilled or more experienced person serves as a role model, teaches, and encourages . . . a less skilled or less experienced person for the purpose of promoting the latter's personal [and professional] development." In addition to professional development, there is an important religious and spiritual role that Christian mentors can play in the workplace for both those who are Christians and those who are not. Past research has shown that workplace mentors have significant and salient influences on work-faith integration for workers.[19] Our own research supports these findings. Mentoring relationships are important for both men and women, but research shows that men are more likely to find mentors at work.

Christians in the workplace should look for both those who can act as mentors and those whom they can mentor. Our research shows that men and women who have succeeded in their work have often been helped by having excellent mentors *regardless of the gender of the mentor*. Unfortunately, for a variety of reasons men can be reluctant to mentor women. Generally, people who play mentor roles at work are most comfortable with mentees who are very similar to them. This becomes problematic if there are not many women in leadership roles, because it limits the opportunity for women to have mentors. (The same case can be made for those from other groups that are underrepresented in

---

[19]Monty L. Lynn, Michael J. Naughton, and Steve VanderVeen, "Connecting Religion and Work: Patterns and Influences of Work-Faith Integration," *Human Relations* 64, no. 5 (2011): 675-701.

leadership roles.) But this does not have to be the situation. More senior men can choose to mentor junior women, and the outcome can be beneficial for both mentor and mentee.

Indeed, male mentors have been highly important in our own professional lives, and neither of us would have had the careers we have had if not for women *and* men who championed us along the way, from dissertation advisers to deans, provosts, university presidents, pastors, and senior colleagues who encouraged our respective leadership gifts in our universities. Elaine remembers a college mentor, a man, who told her that she might want to go to get a PhD. And it was her pastor, also a man, who encouraged her to lead a ministry on faith and science at her church. Denise was encouraged by two of her deans, both men, to pursue leadership roles within her university as well as in the local business community. One of them provided funding and course releases that allowed her to further hone her own skills. There have been many situations where both of us benefited from the efforts of men in our lives who mentored and helped us. In many cases, these men were willing to meet with us individually to provide support, guidance, feedback, and encouragement.

In the previous chapter we talked about how the Billy Graham rule can limit the interactions between male pastors and women in their congregations. But the expression of this rule can also be found in the workplace among Christian men in a way that at best is maladaptive and at worst may be illegal. Both Elaine and Denise have been in situations where men declined to meet with us individually because they were concerned about how such a meeting might be viewed or the potential for impropriety. We have some respect for the motivation of these men, but this approach can feel and be limiting to women. At one point, a Christian business executive, who was old enough to be Denise's father, shared with her his realization that if he were not willing to meet with women one-on-one at work, it would impede their ability to advance in his organization. His realization changed his practices, and he began to open his calendar to individual meetings with women, with the goal of mentoring and supporting them in their careers. That particular man eventually became a great friend and mentor to Denise through two decades of her career.

We heard from a few women who found Christian mentors in their workplaces and even occasionally other, more senior women who played this mentor role. "I appreciate that I have been able to express my faith openly with her and that she has shared some of her personal spiritual struggles with me, that I have learned from," a Christian corporate trainer we met said about her director.[20] "So, I appreciate that by having that resource, that I know, to this day, if I am struggling with something, I know I can call her on the phone right now, about personal stuff or work stuff, and she will have a word from the Lord. . . . I just appreciate her for setting the example that she has."

Sometimes we find the best mentors in our own family. Rochelle, the physician we met in the last chapter who attends an evangelical church, told us how difficult it is to ignore religious messages about women not working outside the home.[21] While she said that these messages can be harmful and difficult to escape, in her own story she was able to leave behind the influence of messages from her church community that discouraged her work because of her grandfather, whose faith she respected enormously and who was an incredible support to her. "For me, it was easy to continue [working] and not to take what was going on at the church to heart because my grandfather told me I could do it. And if I know anybody who was a prayin' man, that's him," she said. In effect, she could see through her grandfather's model that work ambition and sincere faith were totally compatible, and he told her and encouraged her that this was the case for both women and men. She

---

[20]See F@W_ST17, Black woman, age 40, corporate trainer, evangelical, interview conducted November 27, 2017.

[21]F@W_ST137, Black woman, age 43, physician, evangelical, interview conducted September 23, 2019.

went on to note that she has been successful in her medical career and is married to a chemical engineer who is highly supportive of her work.

Because of her experiences, Rochelle has definitive views of what needs to be taught by the church in support of women, emphasizing that the support of pastoral leaders is crucial to how others in the congregation view women's work. "I think they need to show us that it is OK to work and work hard. I think they do a great job with men. But I think they need to show that support more for women," she said. "I think when your pastor appreciates the work you do outside of the home, or in the home, the other people appreciate you."

But of course, pastors are not the only ones who can set the tone for supporting women who work outside the home. It is very often close friends or family members who play this role. Elaine remembers that when she had a baby, she and her husband went back to visit a church they had attended when they were younger. An older friend from the church asked what she was going to do with the baby after her parental leave ended. Elaine replied that she was excited she and her husband had arranged for a daycare on campus. The man replied, "Yuck, you are going to put a baby in daycare to go back to work?!" Before Elaine could think of a response, her husband spoke up, saying, "I sure hope Elaine returns to work since she makes half of our family income and makes our lives better through the interesting and important work she does."

Support a healthy rhythm of work and rest. Churches, workplaces, and leaders can sponsor flourishing for all by supporting a healthy rhythm of work and rest. A culture with such a rhythm has benefits, in particular, for women. There has been increasing public discussion about the impact of "grind culture"—working long hours as a marker of success—exploitative workplaces, and systemic inequalities on individual and communal health. There are also discussions in the broader culture about the ways in which collective trauma and burnout are tied to racial, gender, and economic inequality and the toll this takes, especially on those who are consistently engaged in the fight for equality and justice. We want to stress that the conditions of systemic burnout look even more extreme for women who are part of racially/ethnically minoritized groups.

Sometimes it is the very nature of our Christian passion for work and the idea of being called to work that can lead to burnout. In her research on the passion principle—the idea that Americans feel the need to follow their passion and choose jobs they find fascinating, intriguing, or fulfilling—sociologist Erin Cech notes how the concept of pursuing paid work one loves or feels called to can inadvertently foster structural and cultural inequalities as well as burnout. The jobs that men and women feel passionate about tend to be differentiated by long processes of cultural socialization. As a result, women are more "naturally" passionate about care work—jobs that, generally speaking, tend to garner less pay and prestige, such as social work and teaching, for example. We would add that these are also the types of jobs in which people tend to get especially burned out, experiencing stress-induced and work-related exhaustion, cynicism, and inefficacy.[22] The antidote for burnout is following intentional rhythms of work and rest.[23]

Writer Anne Helen Petersen quotes from women who responded to her own writing on worker burnout, showing that burnout can be especially pronounced for women of color:

> As a black woman I feel as if I was were born tired. Every woman in my family has always worked since adolescence almost until the day they died. That's one thing I think is always missing from conversations about women in the workplace. To middle-class white women, work still seems like somewhat of a novelty. I'm an elementary school teacher. My mother was a social worker. My grandmother was a teacher and her mother was a slave. I was born burned out.[24]

---

[22]See Christina Maslach, Wilmar B. Schaufeli, and Michael P. Leiter, "Job Burnout," *Annual Review of Psychology* 52, no. 1 (2001): 397-422.

[23]See Erin Cech, *The Trouble with Passion* (Oakland: University of California Press, 2021).

[24]Anne Helen Petersen, "Here's What 'Millennial Burnout' Is Like for 16 Different People," BuzzFeed News, January 9, 2019, www.buzzfeednews.com/article/annehelenpetersen/millennial -burnout-perspectives.

Another woman quoted by Petersen remarks, "So many times my pastor has had sermons on how 'you can't be a lazy Christian!' and how 'the church was made to be a community, read the book of Acts!' and the subtext of 'you must do all this for others,' which often means you must absolutely devote your emotional self to others in the church."

Part of sponsoring flourishing for women is looking out for the rest of others and, when we have power, creating work systems that are humane for both men and women. It may also mean reallocating workloads to better fit the capacity of workers at different moments of their lives. The Rev. Jennifer Bailey, who leads the Faith Matters Network, explains,

> In the organization I lead . . . we understand care to be the cornerstone of transformational social movements. And when we talk about care, what we're talking about is a form of collective care that recognizes and sees the deep humanity of [others]. . . . An example of collective care is seeing that my sister is struggling at this moment to show up fully because of something that's happening in her life and inviting her into a period of rest, renewal, and reflection, and then stepping in to be able to cover some of the things that she might have on her plate.[25]

There has been recent interest in practices of wellness and focus on self-care. This has been sometimes critiqued as a hyper-individualist turn or faith-lite, and critics have discussed how contemporary spirituality is increasingly sold to consumers through social media and the wellness industry. In the midst of this, we want to see women make individual changes to take care of themselves—and each other—by incorporating and accepting the act of rest, to act against the prevailing norms that often see women working as second best. But we also need to cultivate collective practices in our churches and workplaces that allow for a more rhythmic and sustainable pace of life.

---

[25]See "From Self-Care to Collective Care," *Religion Unmuted* (podcast), with Jennifer Bailey, July 30, 2021, https://religionunmuted.libsyn.com/from-self-care-to-collective-care. And see Faith Matters Network, https://faithmattersnetwork.org/, for more information about the network Bailey leads.

SPONSOR FLOURISHING FOR ALL

We need to find ways within our church congregations to recognize every person as made in God's image and worthy of the opportunity to develop their God-given gifts. Within our organizations we should be attentive to practices that may limit the opportunities for any group of people, including women, young people, singles, and so on. We know that societies have patterns of inequality that give some groups greater advantages and resources than others, whether in the workplace, home, politics, law, economics, or religious institutions. Society-wide, we have unequal distributions of power based on gender, but this is counter to the example in Scripture. In short, we do not want in our churches and work organizations to "do gender" in a way that creates or reinforces unequal opportunities in everyday life.

As we have discussed, the jobs that men and women feel passionate about tend to be differentiated by long processes of cultural social-ization, and this socialization is often echoed in the church envi-ronment, communicating the message that women belong in caring professions where they can use their gifts to serve others. As a result, women gravitate toward work in service industries—jobs that, gen-erally speaking, tend to garner less pay and prestige and give fewer opportunities for advancement. In our desire to sponsor the servan-thood mentality (a good thing) we may inadvertently deny women opportunities to lead and men opportunities to serve.

As Christians in a variety of workplaces and as pastoral leaders in congregations, we should help women express their giftings both in the church and at work. In the church it is not enough to offer theological support to women's paid labor. There needs to be a practical outworking of this principle in everyday kinds of activities, from sermon examples, to volunteer opportunities, to providing church gatherings for women during off-work hours, to a willingness and intentionality for pastors to meet with women in one-to-one settings. Our workplaces too should be places where women and men are encouraged to develop and express their giftings of service and leadership. We should be attentive to opportunities to mentor and be mentored. And to the extent we have power to do so, we should cultivate rhythmic practices of work and rest for women in particular, but really—as we will discuss in chapter twelve—for everyone.

Our research and that of other scholars reveals that integration between faith and work produces tremendous benefits for worker well-being, satisfaction, and commitment. Unless churches take measures to ensure those benefits are equally available to men and women as the doctrine of the *imago Dei* insists, Christians will continue to contribute to gender inequity.

REFLECTION QUESTIONS

For everyone

- At work, what are practices you can adopt to consistently remind yourself that every person is made in God's image, that every person is worthy of the opportunity to develop their God-given gifts?
- Think about potential workplace mentors—both men and women—who have been successful at work and who have integrated their faith with their approach to work. How could you seek opportunities for a mentoring relationship with these people, regardless of whether they are men or women?
- Think about those at work—both men and women—who could benefit from your workplace knowledge and experience. How could you seek opportunities to mentor these people, regardless of whether they are men or women?
- What things can you do to ensure that men and women have equal opportunities within your organization?
- If you are an organizational leader, how could you better address organizational structures that are gendered and within your

purview? This could include ways assignments are distributed, travel expectations, and where meetings are held.

For faith communities

- To what extent do the examples in sermons and Bible studies reflect the full range of congregational representation with respect to gender roles at work? If they do not, are there ways you could encourage change?

- Who is selected for what kinds of roles in your church? Is there a gendered difference, for example, between who teaches Sunday school versus who is on the budget committee? Do you think the norms and assumptions in your congregation about which gender does what limit the spiritual growth for women and men? If so, are there ways you could encourage change?

10

TALKING ABOUT CHRISTIAN FAITH

Therefore go and make disciples of all nations, baptizing them
in the name of the Father and of the Son and of the Holy Spirit,
and teaching them to obey everything I have commanded you.
And surely I am with you always, to the very end of the age.

MATTHEW 28:19-20

ELAINE FOUND HERSELF on a Greyhound bus traveling between Salt Lake City, Utah, and Bozeman, Montana, to be part of a wedding in a wheat field. She had just started graduate school and was using the time to read *The Elementary Forms of Religious Life*, a sociological classic written by the great French sociologist Emile Durkheim and required reading for the course she was taking in her PhD program. The man sitting beside her worked as a janitor and spent his evenings cleaning schools. Elaine was inspired when he said that as he worked, he would pray over the rooms where the children and the teachers would be the next day. He also used the opportunity to "share the gospel," as he put it, with the people who worked with him. Seeing she was reading a book on religion he asked, "Has anyone ever told you the gospel?" She replied that she was a Christian, and the man then pressed her to tell him what the "gospel really means to you." Over an hour of nonstop conversation later, and less inspired now, Elaine, drawing from her Baptist background, said that the gospel meant "I have been washed in the blood of the Lamb and I know that Jesus Christ has forgiven my sins." He finally seemed convinced, and she, feeling that the surety of her faith was being vetted by someone who did not know her well, felt just plain tired.

Denise, on the other hand, recalls an experience with an Uber driver a few years ago that was quite different. She was returning from an out-of-town interview that would lead to a job offer in another state, and she was wrestling with the decision, weighing the pros and cons of accepting the job and moving her family. Her driver, an Eritrean immigrant to the United States, asked where she had been and what she had been doing, and Denise explained the purpose of the trip and the decision ahead of her. The driver then shared that he was a Christian and asked whether she was too. When Denise acknowledged that she was, the driver spent the next thirty minutes sharing how he had seen God's power and direction in his own life, and asking thoughtful questions that helped her weigh the factors in her own situation a little differently than she had before. When he dropped her off, he summarized his thoughts by noting the value that Jesus placed on little children and encouraging her to ask her own children what they thought of the potential move. He did not try to convince Denise of a particular faith perspective, unlike the man in Elaine's case, but instead shared his faith in a natural and winsome way. As a result of the conversation, Denise felt a sense of God's direction and care rather than the sense of exhaustion Elaine felt on the Greyhound bus.

In this chapter, we focus on how Christian workers see sharing their faith verbally at work—what some call proselytizing—as the principal way they integrate their faith with their work, and we examine the potential upsides and downsides of such an approach to integrating faith and work.

CONCERNS ABOUT HOW TO SHARE

Christians often feel that evangelizing others is one of the most important things we can do to share our faith. We are Great Commission people: we want to spread the gospel to all nations and want Jesus to be known to the ends of the earth. Our research findings show that workers who overtly express their faith at work often worry a lot about how their faith expression might affect others. "So, I've had some patients who say, 'Please stop with all the God stuff. I don't wanna hear that,' and I don't push it [laughs]. I just take cues off people, and instead of forcing it, ask patients, 'Is it OK?'" a physician told us.[1] "A lot of times I'll bring up different scriptures that I've heard and that I've read that have been meaningful to me, or I'll point people to that as a source of encouragement for them" rather than being so overt about it, said a Catholic tax accountant.[2] "A lot of times they're not really Christians, or they're not practicing, but if it comes up in conversation and it seems like I'm being led in that direction," she will talk about her faith, she said. "I don't just, like, get my Bible out and start thumping it at people!"

A civil engineer we met earlier told us she knows her five coworkers well and they mean a lot to her, but she is also aware that she is the most outspoken Christian among them and that the small size of her office means there is very little room for tension.[3] "I guess I deeply feel that I need to talk about my faith at work to some extent because I care about my coworkers, and I think if I truly care about them then that concern has to extend to their spirituality, not just things besides that," she said, but she has struggled with how to express care for her colleagues via her faith without "bugging them."

---

[1] F@W_ST137, Black woman, age 43, physician, evangelical, interview conducted September 23, 2019.
[2] F@W_ST03, White woman, age 50, income tax preparer, Catholic, interview conducted October 23, 2018.
[3] F@W_ST31, White woman, age 25, civil engineer, evangelical, interview conducted December 19, 2018.

WHO EXPRESSES FAITH VERBALLY

In our survey, 42 percent of workers agreed with the statement, "My faith/ spirituality helps me experience meaning and purpose in my daily work tasks," and 22 percent of workers said they are motivated to talk about their faith or spirituality in the workplace—but this desire varies greatly by religious tradition. When we asked workers whether they "feel motivated to talk about [their] faith or spirituality with people at work," we found that 54 percent of evangelical Protestants said they "strongly agree" or "agree," a much higher percentage than in any other religious group. This should come as no surprise, since to be an evangelical is to focus on sharing the good news of Christ and the Christian faith with the hopes that the hearer will also come to believe.[4] (Incidentally, it was not just Christians who were motivated to evangelize their fellow workers. We also found that 28 percent of Muslims said they have a desire to do so.)

Those who feel motivated to talk about their faith or spirituality with people at work by religious tradition

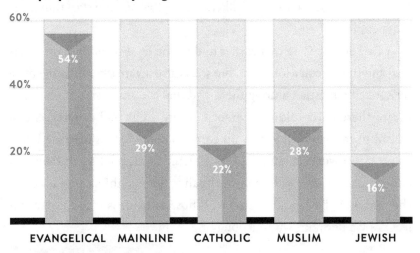

Data: Faith at Work Main and Supplementary Surveys

Figure 10.1

---

[4]See "Evangelicalism," Wikipedia, accessed December 5, 2024, https://en.wikipedia.org/wiki /Evangelicalism.

Our survey also finds racial differences in workplace religious expression. We find that 35 percent of Black workers agreed that they are motivated to talk about their faith with people at work, compared with 26 percent of White workers and 16 percent of Asian workers. Even after accounting for other factors, such as differences in religiosity and religious tradition, Black workers were still more likely than White workers to say they feel motivated to talk to others about their faith while at work.[5]

Those who feel motivated to talk about their faith or spirituality with people at work by race

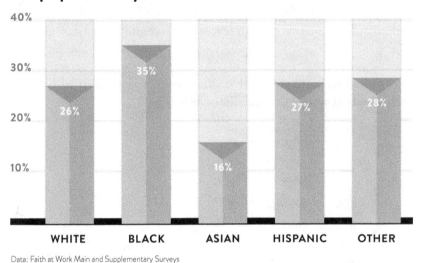

Data: Faith at Work Main and Supplementary Surveys

Figure 10.2

Talking about faith at work also differs somewhat by industry, according to our findings. Unsurprisingly, those who work as pastors or for faith-based nonprofits or churches are more likely than those in other jobs to say they express their faith at work, with 71 percent telling us they feel motivated to talk about their religion in the workplace. (Although

---

[5]Faith at Work Main Survey. If we estimate an ordinary least squares regression model predicting agreement with the statement, "I feel motivated to talk about my faith or spirituality with people at work," we find a statistically significant difference between White and Black workers even after controlling for religiosity, religious tradition, gender, organizational size, and position in organization.

71 percent is high, we wondered why the percentage was not higher given that the nature of these occupations *is* actually to talk about faith.) When we compare other industries, the differences in worker motivation to discuss faith at work are more modest, although they do exist, with those in labor roles somewhat more motivated to talk about religion at work than are those in professional roles. At the higher end are workers in caretaking (34 percent), farming (32 percent), and construction (32 percent), and at the lower end are workers in the arts (23 percent), computer industry (23 percent), the legal sector (21 percent), and the sciences (16 percent). Even when we account for other factors— including religiosity, religious tradition, race, gender, organizational size, and position in the organization—these industry-level differences remain.

Those who feel motivated to talk about their faith or spirituality with people at work by occupational industry

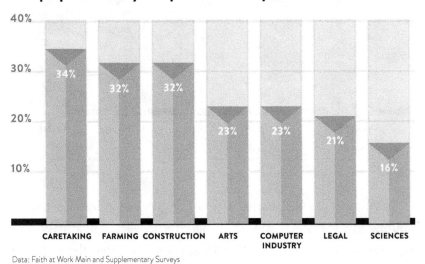

Data: Faith at Work Main and Supplementary Surveys

Figure 10.3

PROFESSIONS WHERE IT IS HARD
TO TALK ABOUT FAITH

As noted above, workers in the tech, legal, and scientific industries are the least likely to say they feel motivated to talk about their faith at work.[6] We think there might be something unique to the cultural logic of these sectors: these professions are perceived as secular, draw people who are more likely to be secular, and are perceived by Christians as being more hostile to expressions of faith.

There are findings that support this idea. Scientists in the United States are less religious than the general population, and research suggests the culture of science can create an environment that makes religious individuals feel like outsiders who are discriminated against because of their faith. Elaine and her colleagues have spent the past twenty years studying how religion shows up in scientific workplaces, and they find that, under certain conditions, the scientific environment can be openly hostile toward religion and expressions of faith. Some individuals we spoke with discussed this.[7] A Christian who manages a scientific lab, for example, said she thinks there are "a few people in the laboratory who I know go to church regularly and are Christian, [Muslim], Catholic, or whatever. But they just—you don't cop to it, in the lab."[8] She said, "People just make comments about, 'Oh, that's so dumb. Christians are this, Christians are that.' Or like, 'Anyone who believes in God is stupid.' It's not directed at a specific person, but I can imagine, especially the friends in the lab that I have that I know are very religious, I'm sure it stings a bit." After hearing how her coworkers speak about people of faith, she is tentative about expressing her religious identity in the workplace.

---

[6]This is based on an ordinary least squares regression model predicting agreement with the statement, "I feel motivated to talk about my faith or spirituality with people at work." The "not applicable" response is coded as "strongly disagree." Other controls in the model include religiosity, religious tradition, race, gender, organizational size, and position in the organization. Note that workers could identify their organization as being in multiple industries, so there is no reference or comparison category. Rather, all industries are included as dichotomous indicators representing whether the individual selected it as one of the industries representing the organization they work for.

[7]See, for example, Christopher P. Scheitle and Elaine Howard Ecklund, "Perceptions of Religious Discrimination Among U.S. Scientists," *Journal for the Scientific Study of Religion* 57, no. 1 (2018): 139-55; see also Elaine Howard Ecklund, *Science vs. Religion: What Scientists Really Think* (New York: Oxford University Press, 2010); Christopher P. Scheitle, *The Faithful Scientist: Experience of Anti-religious Bias in Scientific Training* (New York: New York University Press, 2024).

[8]F@W_ST91, White woman, age 24, lab manager, mainline, interview conducted June 27, 2019.

WHAT CHRISTIANS ARE SHARING

When we asked Christians how they might talk about their faith at work, we sometimes heard about efforts at proselytizing. Several workers we spoke with described to us how they shared their faith to directly or indirectly create opportunities to evangelize to others. While this can be unwelcome, it is generally allowable by the law.[9] "As we're talking to foresters, as we're talking to landowners, I end up sharing . . . why I believe what I believe. And then . . . in that way, opening the subject to be able to witness to them," said a Christian who owns a logging company.[10] "A lady I had worked with for a number of years . . . we were working on our computers," shared a corporate trainer who attends a largely Black Pentecostal church.[11] "She kept looking up, and she's like, 'Can I talk to you for a minute?' This woman was basically like, 'I want to be a Christian' . . . and I led her to Christ, outside the back of the building." Her coworker "saw enough from me to say, 'You know what? I know, if anybody has an answer to what I'm feeling, it's gonna be [you],'" she said. "And that blessed my heart so much." According to an evangelical man who works as a farmer, in some ways it is important for Christians to be completely open about "the things that they believe because [their faith] does touch all aspects of our life. . . . We try very hard to be very open about our Christianity and our faith. And hopefully, everyone who leaves has at least heard a little bit. . . . We try to bring all the conversation around to the why—why we do what we do and why we believe what we believe."[12]

Examples of Christians talking about their faith in the pejorative sense of proselytizing others were in the minority. Generally, we found

[9]See Raymond F. Gregory, *Encountering Religion in the Workplace: The Legal Rights and Responsibilities of Workers and Employers* (Ithaca, NY: Cornell University Press, 2011).

[10]F@W_ST33, White man, age 48, co-owner of logging company, evangelical, interview conducted January 8, 2019.

[11]F@W_ST17, Black woman, age 40, corporate trainer, evangelical, interview conducted November 27, 2018.

[12]F@W_ST87, White man, age 35, farmer, evangelical, interview conducted June 14, 2019.

that forcing faith on others was rarely the intent. More often, when religious individuals talk about their faith at work, they are not trying to convert others but rather express spiritual support or gratitude for their coworkers, a type of faith expression they think can make an organization a more caring place for workers. Some Christians insert comments about their faith into otherwise casual conversation, allowing their coworkers to decide whether the comment will lead to further discussion of faith.

"I guess it comes out most in my development of relationships with coworkers," a data analyst who described herself as a nondenominational Christian said when asked about sharing her faith in the workplace.[13] A woman who works as a director of a medical nonprofit and who attends a church that also has a health care clinic said she aims to "leave the door open" but tries hard not to force anything on anyone: "[If] somebody asks a question about health care, I'll say something like, 'Oh, our church has a clinic, and it's two days a week, for people who are underinsured or uninsured.' And they'll be like, 'Oh, tell me more about that.' So, I'll tell them more about the clinic, and then, if they're interested in the church, then I'll tell them about the church."[14] This director casually slips a faith comment into discussion. The way she frames it allows people to decide whether the comment will lead to further discussion about faith.

A Christian woman who works as a wedding coordinator said that she most often talks about her faith as a way to offer to pray for those she works with when they are going through difficulties.[15] "If somebody shares with me a hard time or something that's happening, sometimes if it's appropriate or if we're in the right place, I will ask if I can pray with them right then and there, and then I do that," she said. "And then

---

[13]F@W_ST77, White woman, age 22, data analyst, evangelical, interview conducted June 3, 2019.
[14]F@W_ST47, Black/Native American woman, age 63, executive director of nonprofit/nurse, evangelical, interview conducted January 31, 2019.
[15]See F@W_ST60, White woman, age 53, wedding coordinator, evangelical, interview conducted February 28, 2019.

I will pray with them, you know, pray for them on my own, and you know, maybe send them texts of encouragement or whatever. Sometimes . . . I'll take them a meal or just send them a card or something like that."

An engineer who works as a program manager said that in most of the places where he has worked, Christians who express their faith are simply naming their sense of thankfulness and attributing it to God rather than having in-depth theological conversations about the gospel.[16]

> I've been in . . . places where you'll hear someone say, "Oh, it was such a blessing to me to be able to work." It's said in a way, and I try to say that myself, you know, if something good comes my way or . . . someone is thanking me for something, you know, I try to express in it a way where it shows that I realize . . . God is in control of all this. So it's just a blessing to me that this person crossed my path or I labor to work with that person.

A man who works as a nurse said that whenever anyone—especially another person of faith—mentions God, he tries to pick up on the mention and amplify it.[17] "I come out of the room, and someone says, you know, 'Thank God.' . . . I acknowledge it. Spirituality definitely is important. If people acknowledge their faith or need someone to acknowledge it with them, then I'm a part of it," he said.

Among the Christian workers we interviewed, there was a lot of reflection on the strength of their relationships with coworkers and whether they were close enough to share their faith. A Christian pediatrician we interviewed, for example, had thought deeply about how she talks about her faith.[18] How she brings up faith in her workplace really "depends on the situation and it depends on people. How close you are to somebody because, like I said, I've talked to a few people

---

[16]F@W_ST09, Black man, age 50, program manager, Black Protestant/Baptist, interview conducted November 2, 2018.

[17]F@W_ST32, White man, age 38, nurse, Catholic, interview conducted December 19, 2018.

[18]F@W_ST56, Asian woman, age 35, pediatrician, evangelical, interview conducted February 20, 2019.

about religion, just whenever it comes up, and so it's not necessarily with everybody, and I think we talk about it sort of not in a judgmental or anything way." She told us that the relationships she has with her coworkers in the medical practice where she works are different from those she has with patients. "I have struggled sometimes bringing up religion with my patients because that's sort of a different relationship," she said, "but if I know that they are religious, sometimes I will bring up things that I think might help them." In essence, this pediatrician is thinking about how other people might receive and react to what she says regarding religion.

A high school ROTC instructor expressed a similar sentiment about how important relationships are to talking about his faith.[19] He said that in one sense he "knows what the answer is, biblically. I know what the right answer is, that I should tell you. And that is, you should express your faith, and you should be proud to be a Christian, and you should—I know that's the right answer." But then he maps this framework onto his situation as an instructor for teens. "The reality is," he said,

> I'm trying to establish a link with my students and a bond of trust, not to bring myself down to their level but to see me as a source of counsel that they can confide in. And if I pigeonhole myself too much into bein', well, "That's the religious guy, that's the religious guy," there's gonna be a segment of those kids who could be turned off by that. Or there's gonna be a segment of parents who could say, "Hey, just watch it. He's one of those religious people," this and that. And, you know, I don't say that negatively, but I wanna impact every kid I can. I wanna impact the atheist kid. I wanna impact the—the Christian kid. So, while I won't deny my faith, if I'm asked, while I won't deny bein' a Christian, I will not push it on them. I won't advertise it, but I will absolutely employ my faith in the line of my duties.

Some Christians discussed expressing faith more through their actions than explicit talk about their faith or evangelism. A man who

---

[19]F@W_ST37, White-Hispanic man, age 43, high school ROTC instructor, evangelical, interview conducted January 10, 2019.

now works as a pastor but previously worked in a context that was not faith-based said that he thinks the way people express their faith in most work environments should be about behavior.[20] "Since I met the Lord I believe that the behavior of a Christian is very different from the behavior of the rest of the people," he said.

> Just like heaven is so far from hell and they are so different, the same should apply to the difference between a Christian and the rest of the people. So, I tried not to respond to teasing. People make fun of you, people are always criticizing. I remained in silence and, whenever I had the chance, I invited someone to go to the church. . . . I was quite a smoker for eleven years, and when I quit smoking people followed my example. They asked me, "How did you do it?" "Well, searching for the Lord," I told them. And that's how I won some persons [over].

A program manager said, "I do say [things about my faith] on occasion."[21] But whether he shares something explicit about his faith "depends on if something is said to me or regarding something, I do—I personally will say, 'Oh, OK, well that's just a blessing.' I don't wear anything, and that's just because of my own personal belief that 'live it versus trying to show it with a symbol,' so I don't really go out of my way to try to have a cross or anything like that." A public-school teacher who said she works in a context where she cannot talk openly about her faith said, "I could teach them Spanish and I could, you know, express Jesus with my lifestyle, but I couldn't talk to them about Jesus the way I can in the environment that I'm in right now."[22] In her case, it is not necessarily a choice to express her faith through her actions but a way that she can still bring people to Christ without directly speaking of religion or breaking job rules and norms.

---

[20]F@W_ST147, Hispanic man, age 58, pastor, evangelical, interview conducted October 16, 2019.
[21]F@W_ST09, Black man, age 50, program manager, Black Protestant/Baptist, interview conducted November 2, 2018.
[22]F@W_ST21, White woman, age 25, Spanish teacher, evangelical, interview conducted December 3, 2018.

THE IMPACT OF SHARING THE FAITH

When Christians talk about their faith sincerely and sensitively, it can be an encouragement for other Christians in the workplace to do the same, leading to a more open and collegial environment for discussions about religion. But Christian expressions of faith in the workplace can also make other workers, especially those from other religious traditions or no religious tradition, feel uncomfortable or marginalized.

We found that many workers from a variety of faith traditions or who are nonreligious worry that any expression of Christian faith in the workplace will lead to widespread proselytization. Many of them also worry that their own faith (or lack thereof) will not be respected by Christians in the workplace. Workers who are not evangelical Christians often mentioned evangelicals as a group they are particularly concerned will push their faith on others. "A lot of my coworkers are religious. . . . So, a lot of times, they will project that to you, and they'll say, 'God bless,' and stuff like that. 'Let's pray.' . . . So, they try to incorporate it into the workplace, and it becomes very uneasy for me, uncomfortable," said a nonreligious security guard who spoke with us.[23] "I feel like they don't see—they don't accept that other people might have different points of view from them. . . . And it could get very uncomfortable at times. It's like they try to force it on to you."

When we asked a Jewish woman who works as a statistician whether she feels comfortable expressing her faith at work, she said,

> Well, that's such a good question. Um, [sighs] I'm realizing through your questions that there's also maybe a difference between expressing your religious affiliation and expressing faith. I will honestly say that I am much more comfortable with talking about people's cultural practices, religious affiliations, holidays, foods, and cultural expressions than I am about faith. . . . Possibly because I don't think many conservative Jews use this language, but I feel

---

[23]F@W_ST200, Hispanic man, age 42, security guard, nonreligious, interview conducted May 3, 2021.

kind of uncomfortable when people tell me to "have a blessed day," right, which feels very Christian, to me. That's not—that is not a way that we tend to talk, and [laughs] it makes me a little uncomfortable. So, that expression of faith in the workplace, when it's on the bottom of an email signature or something like that, I feel distinctly put off.[24]

To her, there was a difference between verbal expressions of faith directed at her and expressing faith through religious symbols. For example, she said: "Now, if somebody wanted to have a little mini-Christmas tree or Christmas lights at their cube, it's not my space. That's fine! I can deal with that."

Some Christians feel their religious identity is not welcome in the workplace. For example, a woman who has a picture of the pope and a necklace with a picture of Jesus on her desk said, "For some reason I feel, because I'm Christian, it's OK [for others] to mock me more. I'm starting to feel in the workforce that they are trying to do diversity but at somebody else's expense. And for some reason it's the Christians, to be at our expense."[25] A man who works as a paramedic supervisor discussed how he sees nonreligious people responding to his faith.[26] He does not feel his Christian faith is affirmed in the workplace. As he explained, "people can express their hatred of religion . . . and feel free to do that, right?" he said.

But the moment you come out, and you defend your faith, you are a—you're classified. It—it's harder to come out and just—and say, "This is my faith" sometimes. . . . When the majority of the people you're surrounded by don't understand it, nor do they want to, then, yet they expect you to understand their side. So, it's tough to come out. Does that make sense?

One study led by Brent Lyons, a professor of organization studies, found that Christian workers who felt that their organization required

---

[24]F@W_ST155, White woman, age 41, survey statistician, Jewish, interview conducted November 9, 2019.

[25]F@W_ST169, Hispanic woman, age 45, information systems analyst, Catholic, interview conducted December 5, 2019.

[26]F@W_ST40, White man, age 42, paramedic supervisor, evangelical, interview conducted January 17, 2019.

them to distance themselves from their religious identity experienced a number of negative outcomes at work. These workers were less likely to talk openly about their faith and rated themselves lower on job satisfaction and personal well-being—and they reported a higher likelihood of turnover—than those who felt their organizations were more supportive of diverse opinions and beliefs.

Conversely, those who felt their workplace was more supportive of various religious identities at work were more likely to openly talk about their faith in the workplace and were more satisfied at work than those who did not share their religion in the workplace.[27] Lyons and his colleagues conclude that when employees feel comfortable bringing their social identities to work—including their religious identity—they are less stressed and more committed to their organization.

REFLECTION QUESTIONS

For everyone

- What are ways that overt expressions of faith can lead to tensions in the workplace, especially as the US workforce becomes more religiously diverse?
- What is the workplace culture around talking about faith in your workplace?
- How does and how should that culture shape your approach to talking about your faith?
- What is the best way to share our faith in the workplace in these times?
- In what ways does talking about faith at work shape the workplace experiences of others? How might you become more aware of how others are experiencing faith-related conversations?

---

[27]Brent Lyons et al., "Applying Models of Employee Identity Management Across Cultures: Christianity in the USA and South Korea," *Journal of Organizational Behavior* 35 (2014): 678-704.

For faith communities

- What ways does your church community encourage you to share your faith with others?
- How does the way your church community encourages you to share your faith shape how you view sharing faith at work?

11

LIVING PRINCIPLED PLURALISM

There is neither Jew nor Gentile,
neither slave nor free, nor is there male nor
female, for you are all one in Christ Jesus.

GALATIANS 3:28

THE WORKPLACE IS the primary place most Christians will encounter and interact with people of different religions or who are not religious at all. It can be difficult to know how to appropriately express our faith in an environment that includes those with various religious beliefs and practices outside our own. For example, when we led our focus groups with Christians in Houston, Seattle, and New York, we found that the topic of how to express one's faith while holding space for others to express their faith came up often as something with which Christians struggled. We also heard from Christians who were seeking clarity on how to appropriately talk about their faith in the workplace without being off-putting to others or engaging in behaviors that would violate organizational standards.

"I don't think that we need to pretend that [religion] doesn't exist because that's like saying, 'This person doesn't exist,' . . . because sometimes religion and the person are conjoined at the hip," a woman working in the technology industry told us.[1] "I think it also needs to be a balance so that you're not offensive to others who aren't as religious. . . . I feel like you have to find a balance between making sure that no one else is offended and you're not encroaching on anyone else's space." A consultant who participated in our Texas focus group mentioned that Christians need to pay attention to laws that prohibit discrimination, but those laws do not necessarily tell people how to "profess Christianity or any particular faith—but they allowed us to, on our lunch break, to share with each other."[2] In this consultant's view, "It's not something you can go around proselytizing . . . because there's a diversity of faiths that there has to be a level of respect, you know, for everyone that's there."

Sometimes there are policies in place or resources available in a workplace that help workers of faith appropriately express and practice their faith. Yet often those resources are not well-known, or workers are not encouraged to use them. For example, a director of real estate operations for a university in our Texas focus group said about the campus where he works: "[Faith] would certainly not be discouraged, but I've never seen anything where it would be encouraged. There's a chapel on campus. That's a place that's open. . . . But I've never heard [from my supervisor something like], 'Feel free to go and pray there.'"[3]

ALLOWING EVERYONE TO EXPRESS THE SAME ASPECTS OF THEIR FAITH

People often find it hard to talk openly about their faith in a pluralistic environment for fear of offending others and instead find it safer to rely on expressing religious affiliation through other means such as religious symbols. In his books *Confident Pluralism* and *Learning to*

---

[1] F@W_ST66, Black woman, age 50, tech consultant, evangelical, interview conducted May 16, 2019.
[2] Focus Group Congregant (FGC) 39, consultant, Texas, focus group conducted April 5, 2018.
[3] FGC 42, director of real estate operations for university, Texas, focus group conducted April 5, 2018.

Disagree, legal scholar John Inazu argues that things have gotten worse in some ways.[4] Even though we know as Americans that pluralism is one of our core values, it has become harder and harder to live together peacefully while still holding and expressing our deepest convictions. Inazu argues that we need empathy, humility, and respect to effectively engage with those whose beliefs are different from our own. Rather than either weaponizing law or politics to force conformity, or avoiding conversations altogether with those holding different viewpoints from our own, we need to practice confidently living out our beliefs and engaging in real life relationships that allow others to do the same.

Building on these ideas, we think it is important that organizations ensure that workers are able to express their faith in the same ways and to the same extent, should they want to, regardless of religious affiliation. For example, if Christians are able to talk about their faith in the workplace, then it is important for Christian workplace leaders to make sure Muslims are afforded the same ability. Sometimes religious workers felt that, rather than working to ensure all workers could equally express or practice their faith in the workplace, organizational leaders instead tried to squash expressions of faith altogether.

In Texas, we interviewed a Christian criminal investigator about expressing faith in the workplace who said he felt suppressing rather than accommodating religion is the norm in most workplaces because "I think that we live in a time where it's very unsafe . . . to let people know who you are because you don't know what's acceptable and what's not acceptable. And it changes from day to day. And so you may think that you are just sharing your life . . . with somebody, [but talking about religion] could actually be punitive, or it can be

---

[4]See John D. Inazu, *Confident Pluralism: Surviving and Thriving Through Deep Difference* (Chicago: University of Chicago Press, 2016). See also Inazu, *Learning to Disagree: The Surprising Path to Navigating Differences with Empathy and Respect* (Grand Rapids, MI: Zondervan, 2024).

consequential."[5] As a Black man, he said he knows what it is like to feel different and be treated differently in the places where he has worked. He also feels that while other faiths are "protected" in the workplace, his faith as a Christian "is not necessarily a protected faith and so, as a result, people who have my faith, we just have to put our heads down and try to keep a low profile because at any time somebody could get offended. And then you have to be on the defensive. And you have to justify why you're not all of these labels [and] prejudices that are placed upon us."

A manager of a large tech company who participated in our Washington state focus group said that because he lives in a nonreligious area of the country, there is more of an "enforced neutrality," an erroneous belief that enforcing no religious expression is somehow more neutral than allowing for expression of various religions.[6] He said,

> There's a lot of communication, executive-level communication, about [diversity]—it's interesting because [this enforced neutrality] is often praised as diversity and celebration of, you know, everybody's background, but it has sort of a deadening effect, it works almost in reverse. . . . I wouldn't say that I've ever encountered active discouragement, but I've probably been less forceful about it. . . . I've relied more on finding ways to connect with people and sharing my faith openly with people that I thought were interested in hearing it.

PRINCIPLED PLURALISM IN THE WORKPLACE

Historian George Marsden, who has examined the interaction of Christianity and American culture, writes, "We do not have effective ways to envision the religious and irreligious sharing a common public realm. We do not have an adequate vision of an inclusive pluralism."[7] In light of these things, we urge Christians to lean into

---

[5]F@W_ST49, Black man, age 38, criminal investigator, evangelical.
[6]FGC_09, general manager of large tech company, Washington, focus group conducted January 18, 2018.
[7]George M. Marsden, "A More Inclusive Pluralism," *First Things*, February 2015, www.firstthings .com/article/2015/02/a-more-inclusive-pluralism.

what we call a "principled religious pluralism," which prioritizes the idea of seeing each person as made in the image of God and engaging in a radical embrace of others. Our theological commitments demand this radical embrace, and it is principled in the sense that it demands religious beliefs be lived authentically rather than dumbed down to the lowest common denominator.[8] The concept of principled pluralism was first articulated by Abraham Kuyper, a Dutch politician, journalist, and theologian in the Reformed tradition who became prime minister of the Netherlands in the early 1900s. Kuyper advocated for an approach to governing that recognized the rights of those from minority religious communities to use their own belief and value systems to maintain their own institutions and associations, even while participating in the larger project of citizenship in a common state. We are borrowing some of his ideas and translating them to our increasingly religiously pluralistic workplace culture.

Principled pluralism starts with the assumption that some individuals or groups may have religious beliefs and practices that are different from those around them. The "others" may be from other religious traditions or no religious tradition. Principled pluralism does not require anyone to let go of their own beliefs or practices or even to concede that all beliefs and practices are equally valid, but it does require an equal value placed on the human worth and dignity of each person, regardless of their faith tradition. Principled pluralism compels Christians to know and stand up for the particulars of their faith while also coming to know the differing particulars of others' faiths. This approach requires a willingness to be open to the idea that others' beliefs and practices may have real value to them and to their communities. Even if you may not fully understand another religion, principled pluralism acknowledges that each person has access to

---

[8]See for a general discussion of religious pluralism Neelam Bano, Humaira Ahmad, Javaria Hassan, and Rafia Razaq, "Principles of Religious Pluralism," *Religions* 14, no. 1 (2023): 20.

common grace and that non-Christian religions may mediate God's grace in some way.

Principled pluralism is not privatization of religion. It does not require a polite separation of one's religion from the rest of one's life in the public square. Rather, it requires a clear understanding of one's *own* beliefs and practices, and a willingness and ability to express them. It places a high value on truth telling as each person understands truth. At the same time, principled pluralism is not coercive. It does not try to win the argument or undermine the beliefs of the other person. Instead, it is expressed through a strong sense of humility, recognizing that we all are limited and can learn from the values, perspectives, and perhaps even the religious commitments of others.

Finally, principled pluralism means we value justice and treating others fairly. It therefore means that we usually provide support for the expression or practice of beliefs that are different from our own. While we may not necessarily agree with others, we will seek to understand as fully as possible the beliefs and practices of others and to treat those who hold them with full respect and dignity. This involves taking the time to be in relationship with others, listening carefully to them, and getting to know the ideas and values that animate their lives, while remaining connected to our own core Christian beliefs and practices. Our data show that many of our respondents but particularly evangelical Christians are likely to report that the people they work with have influenced their thoughts about faith (see fig. 11.1). This suggests that conversations about faith are happening with workplace colleagues and that many of these conversations are reflective of an openness to learning from others.

Here we borrow from the theologian Miroslav Volf's idea of "the drama of embrace," where we start, in this case, with a metaphorical "opening of the arms."[9] We then enter into a posture of "waiting," where

---

[9]See Miroslav Volf, *Exclusion and Embrace: A Theological Exploration of Identity, Otherness, and Reconciliation* (Nashville: Abingdon, 2019).

Those who agree that the people they work with have influenced their thoughts about faith

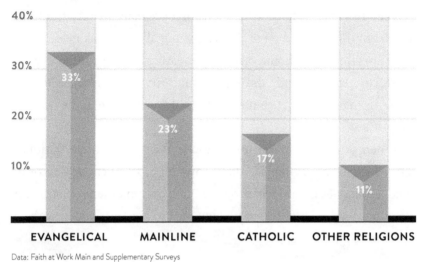

Data: Faith at Work Main and Supplementary Surveys

Figure 11.1

we are not imposing ourselves on others but are reaching out for reciprocity and allowing others to come. Then there is the "closing of arms," where there is mutual interaction and exchange around one another's ideas and practices. It is important, warns Volf, that our embrace is not too tight, that it allows for the agency of the other. Then we have an "opening again," which allows each party to keep its full identity.

We like the idea of incorporating radical embrace in the concept of principled pluralism since it allows us as Christians to hold firm to our own theological convictions and principles while also recognizing and honoring the moral value of each person in a pluralistic setting because each one of us—from our Christian standpoint—is created in the image of God. Because Christians who practice this approach must also be committed to the covenantal identity we have in Christ, we are able to fully share the best version of our Christian faith. While we do so, we also engage in a pluralistic environment where we recognize the value in the faiths of others, with neither side expecting faith to be watered down to the lowest common denominator. Christian workplace leaders should continue to think about how they can advocate for others and protect the rights of those who are from more marginalized traditions as part of their overall ethic of recognizing all people as made in the image of God. They should take extra measures to care for the "least of these," to make sure that those from minority religious traditions get what they need to practice their faith in the workplace in the way that they desire.

When principled pluralism is practiced across an organization, it should result in a workplace that allows for a broad expression of religion, that does not prioritize one religion over another, is not institutionally coercive, and does not allow for individual coercion with respect to religion.

POWER DYNAMICS

Power is an important dynamic to attend to in discussions of principled religious pluralism. In many workplaces, there is unequal religious accommodation and expression: those in the religious majority or in roles of authority often experience greater religious freedom, and it is often more difficult for workers of minority faiths or in less powerful positions to request the same allowances. For example, Elaine remembers meeting with a friend who was the CEO of a large corporation to discuss his work. He told her that he always starts his staff meetings with prayer. When she asked him whether those in his organization, which included Hindus, atheists, and Muslims in addition to Christians, were bothered by the prayer, he said, "No, they all really love it." She wondered whether this was really the case or whether some in the staff meetings felt marginalized but were too afraid to say anything because of the power the CEO had over their work lives.

A woman who works as a financial analyst told us about having a party for her Christian boss where family members of the boss criticized her because she did not start the party with prayer.[10] She explained herself by acknowledging that even though she is a committed Christian, she is "sensitive to the fact that everybody in the room might not be on board, but then, too, to me, your expression of [faith]; I am not a—a slogan-type Christian person. It should be in what you do. And I don't have to do this to prove to you that I'm a Christian. . . . So, you really live out your faith, in a—in a more substantive way, as opposed to somebody's add-on of activities."

We found that workers from religious minority traditions are often afraid to ask for religious accommodation or to display their faith symbols in the workplace because they fear it might subject them to religious discrimination. Those who are in the religious majority and positions of organizational leadership need to be sure they are not using their power in a coercive way. Practicing a principled pluralism means thinking about what it means to create organizations that thoughtfully accommodate and embrace the religious beliefs of others.

A Jewish man we interviewed who works as a consultant said,

Someone who says, "Well let's have morning prayer," right, as part of our workplace regimen. . . . [Well,] my prayers may be very different from your prayers and who we pray to may be very different. . . . If you're going to be singled out 'cause you're not wanting to pray that prayer to that God or whatever. . . . When you're sort of endorsing or pushing someone into something and saying, "Oh no, now we're also going to have morning prayer 'cause I'm a faith-based person and you all work for me, so let's do morning prayer." Like no, not part of what I think is a good way to have faith in the workplace.[11]

He went on to explain that workplaces could be inclusive of different faiths as long as they take each person's faith perspective seriously. "I'm happy to have that conversation about . . . what's your Easter look like?

---

[10]F@W_ST18, Black woman, age 45, financial analyst, Black Protestant/Baptist, interview conducted November 28, 2018.
[11]F@W_ST108, White man, age 52, consultant, Jewish, interview conducted August 2, 2019.

Here's what my Passover looks like. Let's compare, right. So, I think in terms of learning and understanding traditions, I think that's an OK conversation to have. . . . So, I think there's good and bad ways to have faith in the workplace."

A Muslim man who works in technology told us that his company has broad policies for religious practice but that the religious makeup and culture of his office make it very hard for him to ask for accommodation.[12] He said there are simply not enough Muslims in his workplace, and among them not enough who would like to practice the daily prayers like he does, to support setting aside space for his religious practice. While there are rooms that his management says Muslims can use for prayers, those rooms are used for many different purposes, which makes it hard to use them as prayer rooms during the workday. Christians in the workplace practicing principled pluralism would be concerned about this impediment to faith expression in the workplace and try to advocate for the right situation for their Muslim colleagues.

Principled pluralism will look different in different types of work environments. Some organizations are not religiously pluralistic by design. That is, they may have a faith-oriented mission and hire workers only from a particular faith tradition. For example, Denise has worked in Christian higher education for nearly thirty years, and in these religious-based organizations, principled pluralism would be largely about acknowledging different approaches to the Christian tradition. Elaine, on the other hand, has worked in secular private and state universities during her career, where there is a much more religiously diverse group of employees, and principled pluralism would involve those various faith traditions. Similarly, the experiences of a worker in a Christian nonprofit or small, privately owned company with a faith-oriented mission are likely to be different from someone who works for a large,

---

[12] F@W_ST148, Asian man, age 42, technical staff, Muslim, interview conducted October 17, 2019.

publicly traded company or a government organization. As a child services specialist—who said he tries to find ways to respectfully talk about his faith with others—told us, how faith is talked about in the workplace "depends on who you work for and what your job is. My job is for the government, you know," he said.[13] "I believe in the Constitution and the division of the government from faith, so I'm not actively out there promoting my beliefs through my job, but maybe—if you worked at some other jobs where you're maybe in the private sector—I think that you should have a little bit more latitude in that."

INCLUDE RELIGION IN DIVERSITY TRAINING

Christian workers we spoke with mentioned that they sometimes wished they knew more about other faith traditions beyond Christianity. Rarely, however, is religion included in diversity, equity, and inclusion trainings. "Sometimes, it's referencing a cultural group, like the Muslims, because they're using that as a cultural group versus a religious thing. But, no," said a woman who works as an educational consultant when asked whether religion comes up in trainings on diversity in her workplace.[14] A senior analyst for a natural gas marketing company told us that in her workplace, diversity experts have referenced religion "as part of code of conduct. It's just more or less learning to accept people's differences and not taking offense or being offensive to people of other faith or different cultures. More or less teaching you how to be open-minded and respectful . . . not directly, just more or less being respectful."[15]

Many workers felt religion *should* be included in diversity trainings in workplaces as part of creating pluralistic work environments. For

---

[13]F@W_ST171, White man, age 35, child services specialist, evangelical, interview conducted December 6, 2019.

[14]F@W_ST101, White woman, age 73, educational consultant, Catholic, interview conducted July 16, 2019.

[15]F@W_ST30, Black/Hispanic woman, age 47, senior analyst for natural gas marketing, mainline, interview conducted December 18, 2018.

example, a Christian financial analyst said that while her workplace does have diversity training on race and gender, "I don't think I've ever seen anything on religion."[16] She told us the consequences of not having discussions of religion as part of diversity trainings were made clear when her workplace hired someone who is a Sikh. "So . . . that's some new diversity," she said.

> And I was like, "Oh, my gosh!" So, I was more worried about somebody doing something offensive to him [laughs]. . . . We kinda had a discussion about it. I kinda call it my preemptive education about it. I was like, "Look. He's a Sikh. This is what—this is a belief. This is what they do. Google it. Do *not* [laughs] do anything crazy!" Because I have folks who are kinda bold. And, you know, they're like, they would probably touch him or something! And I was like, no. No, no, no, no. Go do your reading before he gets here.

In this way she encouraged her workers to educate themselves about their new coworker's beliefs. Although there was not a diversity training program at her workplace, she was motivated by her Christian faith to see a need for it and filled the gap. She emphasized the necessity of it.

A Jewish man who worked for a state legislature also stressed that diversity trainings in his workplace could include more on religion.[17] In particular, he thought it would be useful to have information about what Orthodox Jews believe or practice so that would not be as surprising. "In a public-facing job, people should have that [kind of training], and whether you're in the Capitol, it's very public-facing, or even in the district, you know, whoever can walk in. I think that it doesn't need to be like sensitivity training specifically, but just an exposure to different beliefs and practices and customs could then help people be more mindful," he said. "Our district has a lot of Sikhs in the district," he added, "and I'm not familiar with their customs. I

---

[16]F@W_ST18, Black woman, age 45, financial analyst, mainline, interview conducted November 28, 2018.
[17]F@W_ST160, White man, age 29, field representative for state legislator, Jewish, interview conducted November 19, 2019.

wouldn't know if it would be considered, you know, disrespectful if I didn't shake someone's hand or something like—it would be very useful to know."

Overall, workplace leaders have a responsibility to chart the way forward in demonstrating nuanced religious accommodation for their employees, including a respect for religious differences, thoughtfulness and willingness to meet the needs of employees' religious traditions, the right spaces for discussions about religion, and intentional care for minoritized groups that have less power in an organization. All of these are necessary for healthy religious pluralism within the workplace. And Christians should be leading the way.

REFLECTION QUESTIONS

For everyone

- What would it mean for you to spend time trying to better understand your coworkers from different religious traditions, as well as those who are not religious, and what they value?

- If you are an organizational leader, how can you help create a workplace in which employees feel comfortable talking about their religious beliefs and practices, and how they shape who they are at work and how they approach their work? What would it look like for you to appropriately model this transparency and vulnerability for others?

- What would it look like for you to stand up for those who are being mocked or ridiculed at work because of some aspect of their religious identity?

- What ways can you think of for Christians to express their faith at work without directly talking about it?

- What are appropriate ways of talking about faith that are self-referential but do not pressure others to convert?

For faith communities

- Do the examples in sermons and Bible studies model ways that Christians could share their faith at work in pluralistic environments?
- Do these examples rely on a range of faith expression—both including and going beyond directly talking about faith?

12

REST

Thus the heavens and the earth were
completed in all their vast array.

By the seventh day God had finished the work he had been
doing; so on the seventh day he rested from all his work. Then
God blessed the seventh day and made it holy, because on it
he rested from all the work of creating that he had done.

GENESIS 2:1-3

For anyone who enters God's rest also rests from
their works, just as God did from his.

HEBREWS 4:10

OUR CHAPTER ON REST has no pairing. There are two reasons for this. First, in some sense all of the previous eleven chapters, which are focused on work, provide a pairing for this chapter on rest. But perhaps more significantly, in each of our pairings, our data that make up the first of the two chapter identify a problem related to faith at work. In the case of rest, our data is actually the *silence*. People did not talk much about rest when we interviewed them about work, and we think folks who want to better integrate their faith and work *ought to be* talking about rest more. So we take that on here.

In the early 1900s, social thinker Max Weber developed the concept of the Protestant work ethic. Weber argued that the belief of predestination in Calvinism—that the fate of one's soul is already determined by God regardless of one's own actions—led believers to feel that the only way to know they were bound for heaven was through evidence of piety and hard work.[1] In this way, then, a person's piety and industriousness functioned to reveal to the self and others evidence of God's (predestined) blessing. This in turn resulted in behavior that manifested as a religiously dedicated work ethic, which proliferated into culture more broadly, giving rise to a rational accounting for money and in turn the spirit of capitalism.

Neither of us ever heard in church the *direct* message that our salvation depended on how hard we worked—in fact, we heard the opposite: that our salvation was a free gift from God and independent of our own efforts. Yet, we nonetheless imbibed an *indirect* message from our culture (and families and churches too!) about the importance of trying to please God through our work. In our research, we heard some workers explicitly or implicitly reference a similar message: that it is our hard work that demonstrates godliness. It is easy to go from hard work as a way of honoring God to hard work as a badge of honor for the self that signals we have a stronger work ethic than others. "Pull yourself up by your bootstraps!" could be the title of an American anthem, pointing to an idea that as individuals we have the power to thrive if only we work hard enough.[2]

We found that Christians we interviewed often used faith to motivate hard work and a sense of accountability, which can have positive

---

[1] Max Weber, *The Protestant Ethic and the Spirit of Capitalism and Other Writings* (New York: Penguin, 2002).
[2] See Joel Kime, "The Dangerous Ideology of 'Pull Yourself Up by Your Bootstraps'—Ezekiel 25–28, Part 4," Engaging Scripture, November 4, 2021, https://joelkime.com/2021/11/04/the-dangerous-ideology-of-pull-yourself-up-by-your-bootstraps-ezekiel-25-28-part-4/.

dimensions. Christian workers tend to view God as sitting on their shoulder whispering things such as, "Keep working" and "Work harder" and "Work with more excellence." A correctional officer said he feels "like I have to always try to be the best at work. . . . I don't try to do better than other people, but I try to be the best that I can be. And I always try to do a really good job. . . . I feel like my faith encourages me to do the very best job that I can, no matter how I'm feeling that day."[3] An administrative assistant said that her faith too "is a huge influence on a very strong work ethic."[4] She told us, "I would say just because I believe everything I do is done unto God, and so it's really important to me to be a good employee, to be on time and to work hard, not to waste my employer's time or money."

Krista, the scientist we spoke with whom we met earlier in the book, said that her faith provides an internal drive to keep working hard even when the work is not exciting: "I think that in little ways [faith] helped me stay motivated because there's some days where it's really cool science . . . and then there are other days where it's in the lab or on my computer trying to do work, and nothing is working, and knowing that I am doing this for a certain goal helps me push through. . . . I think [my faith] kind of helps me be accountable for when I would be more apt to back off or maybe cut corners."[5]

But there are ways that a theologically justified work ethic can have negative dimensions. Many workers, we found, work as hard as they can—sometimes so hard that they struggle with burnout. Sociologists Todd Ferguson and Josh Packard looked at pastors after the pandemic and found that many church leaders feel trapped by the modern forces of declining church membership and the rapidly expanding role of the

[3] F@W_ST11, White man, age 63, corrections officer, evangelical, interview conducted November 8, 2018.
[4] See F@W_ST34, White woman, age 34, administrative assistant, evangelical, interview conducted January 8, 2019.
[5] F@W_ST99, White/Hispanic, woman, age 23, PhD student in marine biology, evangelical, interview conducted July 12, 2019.

pastor.[6] They must be theologians, counselors, organizational leaders, building managers, and more. Like these pastors, everyday church members have taken the verse "I can do all things through Christ who strengthens me" (Philippians 4:13 NKJV) out of context, in a way where the emphasis is on us and the doing rather than on God, the community, and what we are providing for the community. (Incidentally, we found in our data that greater workplace accommodation and support of workers' faith was associated with less frequent burnout.)

We need a different perspective. We need to move to the idea that we work best when we engage in the God-ordained rhythms of work and rest.

It may seem ironic that we end our book on work with a chapter on rest. We end with a discussion of rest partly because, in the biblical story, God ends the activity of creation with rest, and that seems to be a good model to follow. We need to ponder rest because it is the created intent. God could have done it differently, but God created and then rested. It is also important for us to notice that the first full day of activity for humans after their creation on day six (before the fall and sin entered the world) was the day of rest on day seven. If the origin story has the first full day of humanity as a sabbath, then it is part of the created order for us to rest. We also attend to rest because it reminds us of our limitations, and we need a deep sense of our limitations to fully integrate our faith and our work.

But first a caveat: We need to admit that resting well is extremely challenging for both of us. We both have worked as hard as we possibly could during the week not always to serve God but to justify through our hard work the allowance for a sabbath at the end of the week. Both of us have then taken said sabbath in name only, spending hours and hours working in our respective churches or catching up on home chores, in essence shifting our work burden from one domain to

---

[6]See Todd Ferguson and Josh Packard, *Stuck: Why Clergy Are Alienated from Their Calling, Congregation, and Career and What to Do About It* (Minneapolis: Fortress, 2023).

another. Both of us have been so focused on our work that when we got to the end of the day we could not remember when we had last gone to the bathroom or eaten anything. Both of us have tried to fit in "just a little bit more" before heading home from the office, going to bed, or starting the weekend. We both at times have used our vacations to do service trips or to help needy family members in ways that were anything but restful. On more than one occasion, Elaine has ignored physiological imperatives from her body, using a bathroom break as a reward for sitting at the computer for fifteen more minutes. We both identify with workers we surveyed and interviewed who find it hard to slow down.

There is nothing inherently wrong with any of these things. Taken together, however, they reveal the lives of two people who need to be reminded that we are limited and that the world does not ultimately depend on our work. We care so much about rest not because we have figured it out but because we struggle so much to rest well. Like other Christian workers, the ways we have been shaped by our cultural context, our churches, and our families make healthy practices of rest very difficult. We can relate to the T-shirts we've seen with the expression, "I'll rest when I'm dead," and the poem by theologian and therapist Wayne Muller, who writes: "Every swept floor invites another sweeping, every child bathed invites another bathing. When all life moves in such cycles, what is ever finished? The sun goes 'round, the moon goes 'round, the tides and seasons go 'round, people are born and die, and when are we finished? If we refuse rest until we are finished, we will never rest until we die."[7] We need to rest from work because it is practical to do so. "For organizations, burnout contributes to declines in productivity, a more stressed and unhappy workplace, and greater turnover. And it's often an organization's most talented and valuable workers who are most likely to burn out," writes

---

[7]Wayne Muller, *Sabbath: Finding Rest, Renewal, and Delight in our Busy Lives* (New York: Bantam Books, 1999), 83.

organizational expert Alex Soojung-Kim Pang in his book *Rest: Why You Get More Done When You Work Less.*[8] And we need to rest from work because it is right to do so. We need to leave behind the idea that it is our work that makes us whole in God and earns us rest. We need to show the way forward to see rest as a gift from God.

REST TAKES WORK

We believe that never before has the need for rest been more urgent or faced greater impediments. Society is changing faster than ever. With automation, the expectation of speed for most tasks is increasing, and with globalization the entire world is more accessible than ever before. This means that most of us have exposure to more new ideas than before, and we feel busier than ever as we process more and more information. Rest is the perfect antidote to the increasing speed of life. At the same time, rest is more difficult for many of us to engage in due to a variety of historical and cultural factors.

While we might think that the Fourth Commandment's injunction to keep the Sabbath would protect Christians from the accelerating demands of society, the opposite may be true. In our interviews with Christians, most of them never talked about their habits of rest or its importance in their lives. Most of those we interviewed were taught by American society, their family of origin, and their church that being faithful to God means working as hard as possible. Rarely did we hear Christians connect their faith to putting boundaries on work or resting more.

Our "first formation" in our family plays a central role in how we view work, the kind of jobs we take, how we approach work, and how we hold work in tension with the other elements of our lives.[9] For

---

[8]See Alex Soojung-Kim Pang, *Rest: Why You Get More Done When You Work Less* (New York: Basic Books, 2024).

[9]Other scholars and thinkers have talked about the importance of families in the "first formation" process, the first social space in which many of us develop our core values. But we love the treatment of first-family formation related to leadership in Jim Herrington, Trisha Taylor, and R. Robert Creech, *The Leader's Journey: Accepting the Call to Personal and Congregational Transformation* (Grand Rapids, MI: Baker Academic, 2020).

example, what our parents do for their work is likely to shape both what we do for our work and how we approach work.[10]

Some of us get the idea from our families that hard work is even part of godliness. For example, Elaine's grandparents, who helped raise her, had full-time jobs and also ran what they called a "hobby farm" on the side. Their "hobby," at least as it was communicated to Elaine, involved literally backbreaking work (both needed back surgeries in their older age). It sometimes involved getting up early in the morning before their day jobs and working well into the night to feed the animals and put hay in a mow before a summer rain rolled in. Denise's father worked in finance and commuted from the suburbs to the city each day. He would leave early and return just in time for dinner, often doing additional work in his den late into the night. Later in his career, he started his own business, and it was not unusual for him to finish his work just before most restaurants closed so he could stop in and get something to eat on the way home. He viewed his work as something he did to serve God and to honor the talents that God had given him, and Denise remembers both implicit and explicit messages to work hard and do one's best. In short, we were both raised to see hard work as a badge of honor. Both of us took this injunction to work long, hard hours—whether at physical or mental labor—as part of our Christian calling. But, as Pang writes, "When we treat workaholics as heroes, we express a belief that labor rather than contemplation is the wellspring of great ideas and that the success of individuals and companies is a measure of their long hours."[11]

FOCUS ON THE FIXED POINT

Even if you have never been to a ballet, you know what the pirouette is. It is one of the most basic and yet most impressive moves ballerinas do.

---

[10]See Natalie Proulx, "Will You Follow in Your Parents' Footsteps?," *New York Times*, December 1, 2017, www.nytimes.com/2017/12/01/learning/will-you-follow-in-your-parents-footsteps.html.

[11]Alex Soojung-Kim Pang, *Rest: Why You Get More Done When You Work Less* (New York: Basic Books, 2024), 29.

They get on one toe and spin fast. How do they do it without getting really dizzy? There are two key principles. The first is staring at a fixed point. While their bodies move quickly, ballet dancers employ "spotting"; they fix their gaze on a single spot. Focusing on the spot allows them to quickly whip the head around at the end of each turn, minimizing the time the head is rotating. While their bodies move, their gaze comes back to the fixed spot each time.[12]

The second principle is simple but hard. They practice. In the beginning of learning to do the pirouette, ballerinas get dizzy. But over time, their nervous system adapts to the changes and their bodies learn how to stay in and come out of a spin without that feeling. On the way to doing a successful pirouette, there is wobbling and falling. It takes acceptance of the wobbles and the falls along the way to master the move. We bring these lessons about focus and practice to our understanding of how to rest well.

First, we need a complete reorientation of our relationship to work and rest. We are convicted that, even as the world is spinning around us, resting from our work and creating healthy rhythms of work and rest will help us better live out our core values. In essence, rest allows us to fix our gaze on God in the midst of the spin cycle of life. Second, we need specific practices that will help us rest at a variety of different time intervals and in a variety of different contexts over the life course. The practice of resting is far from automatic. It requires a regular and ongoing commitment. It sounds like an oxymoron to say that we should practice rest, but making the decision to rest is only part of the solution.

WORKING ON REST

Thinking of resting in order to work requires a complete shift in mindset. We do not get to rest as a reward *because* we have worked

---

[12]See Amir Kheradmand, "Why Don't Figure Skaters Get Dizzy When They Spin?," *Scientific American Mind* 27, no. 6 (2016): 72, www.scientificamerican.com/article/why-don-t-figure-skaters-get-dizzy-when-they-spin/.

hard. Rather, we rest because it is the created intent to do so and because we are limited. Ultimately, the success of our work does not completely depend on us and how hard we work. As with any job or profession, "you need preparation to be able to do this job, taking time for yourself, because you're not God, you're just a human being," said a pastor we interviewed. "Therefore, we need to rest . . . in addition to praying and doing the things the way Jesus told us."[13]

A man who is the chief financial officer of a credit union told us how his faith provided a sense of rest during the day that changed him from seeing himself in control to acknowledging that God is in control.[14] "If people believe in God or a higher power, I think it helps—or at least for me helps—to maybe relieve that stress, like, OK, there's somebody else that's watching out for me, or there's somebody else that's in control here. This is not just a random series of events that, you know, there's no control over or there's nobody—that something could spiral out of control," he said. "Bad things do happen to people all the time, but I think having a belief in God helps to just not get stressed out as much because you're thinking that there is some plan here and somebody else has some control over it."

Other workers we interviewed also talked about a reorientation to work that helps them understand that God is in control. Recognizing his limits, a correctional officer said he is different from his own father "by believing that God is in charge of everything."[15] He wonders

how people get by without a sound faith in God. My dad was an atheist growing up, and he always said that faith in God was just for the weak, that people who can't take care of themselves put their faith in God and just 'cause they're not strong. And in some ways I almost agree with him because people might look at me outwardly and think that I've always thought of myself as

---

[13]See F@W_ST147, Hispanic man, age 58, pastor, evangelical, interview conducted October 16, 2019.

[14]F@W_ST10, White man, age 59, CFO for credit union, evangelical, interview conducted November 6, 2018.

[15]F@W_ST11, White man, age 63, corrections officer, evangelical, interview conducted November 8, 2018.

ten feet tall and bulletproof, but it isn't because of me, it's because of my faith in God. And so, I really think of myself as a weak person who gets filled up with strength from the Lord.

Elaine has listened to *The Leader's Journey* podcast episode "Leadership and Rest, Sabbath, and Sabbaticals" probably ten times.[16] Here is the central principle: Leaders who rigorously practice rest and who learn to work from rest, not work for rest, move past performance and entitlement and can sustain healthy leadership for the long haul. Rest has practical importance to work as well. Pang, who consults with companies on how to implement a shorter workweek, writes about how companies can better integrate rest into work, using scientific research and examples to show how deliberate rest can make work more creative, productive, and sustainable. As he writes: "If you want rest, you have to take it. You have to resist the lure of busyness, make time for rest, take it seriously, and protect it from a world that is intent on stealing it." In what follows we draw on our research, Christian thinkers, and the tapestry of our own lives to offer practical activities and habits that will help orient us toward rest.

Minute by minute and day by day. As we think about our work and what it means to work from a place of rest, we are convinced that we need more than just a sabbath one day each week. We need practices and rhythms of rest that we inhabit throughout each day. In his book *Working from the Inside Out*, Jeff Haanen, founder of the Denver Institute for Faith & Work, writes, "We were always meant to live the spiritual life in and through our real, daily life."[17] As Denise writes in her book with Shannon Vandewarker, *Working in the Presence of God*, "More than anything we need to learn to fix our gaze on God. We need to restore our orientation to God throughout the day. Doing so requires daily and sometimes even moment-by-moment practices to

---

[16]See "Leadership and Rest, Sabbath, and Sabbaticals," *The Leader's Journey* (podcast), September 29, 2023, https://theleadersjourney.us/leadership-and-rest-sabbath-and-sabbaticals/.

[17]See Jeff Haanen, *Working from the Inside Out: A Brief Guide to Inner Work That Transforms Our Outer World* (Downers Grove, IL: InterVarsity Press, 2023).

shape us toward recognizing God's presence amid our daily work, continually reminding us during our workday to keep our gaze fixed on God."[18]

Daily reorientation practices. One reorienting practice that Denise and Shannon wrote about in their book is creating a "liturgy of commute" that becomes a part of the daily work rhythm. Elaine has been using this practice for years to help her rest in God throughout the day. Most mornings as she walks to work, she prays a rendition of a phrase from Psalm 46: "Be still and know that I am God." She repeats the phrase, "Let me be still and know that you are God" to herself on the early part of her walk to the university campus. She walks quickly as she prays, "Let me be still." When thoughts intrude, reminding her of what she needs to get done in the work hours ahead and what has been left undone in the home hours behind, she prays, "Let me be still." As she gets nearer to the campus, she tries to resist the urge to start a mental litany of the to-do list for her day. "Let me be still." As she waits for the light to change, she stands on one foot and then the other, trying to get in a few balance exercises that her physical therapist told her to do every day after her joint replacement in her toe. "I am easily distracted. Let me be still." Once on campus and through the beautiful entrance with its ornate architecture, her walk takes her through a building-sized art installation, which has a square in the top that is open to the sky. Here she turns to the second part of her prayer, "Let me know that I am loved fully by God." Christian workers can develop their own version of a liturgy of commute that helps orient them to God as they begin their workday.[19]

Breath prayers. An evangelical Christian technology consultant told us he could not get through the day without continually turning to

---

[18]Denise Daniels and Shannon Vanderwarker, *Working in the Presence of God: Spiritual Practices for Everyday Work* (Peabody, MA: Hendrickson, 2019).

[19]See Elaine Howard Ecklund, *Why Science and Faith Need Each Other: Eight Shared Values That Move Us Beyond Fear* (Grand Rapids, MI: Brazos, 2020).

prayer.[20] He said that he "starts the day off in prayer. You know, for knowledge, and I always thank God for how far we've come, open, bless the new day." He then repeats these prayers throughout the day. Haanen writes about "breath prayers" that can be said quietly by Christian workers throughout the office or on the factory floor, such as 1 Samuel 3:10, "Speak, for your servant is listening." Christians can learn from the Muslim tradition, which includes the practice of five daily prayers, in adopting a practice of prayers that might infuse a sense of rest into the workday. As one Muslim social media manager we spoke with said, "When I am able to just stop and go for my five- to ten-minute prayer, I think it's definitely a restart to my day. It's a refresher."[21]

Breath prayers can also be used in times of significant stress and difficulty. When Denise was recovering from open-heart surgery a few years ago, she found herself in the cardiac ICU with fluid buildup in her lungs, difficulty breathing, and dangerously low oxygen levels.[22] While the medical personnel were trying to treat these problems and it became clear that the treatment was going to take hours rather than minutes, the only thing she could think to do was to pray with each breath. As she breathed in, she prayed, "Lord fill me with your spirit." As she breathed out it was, "Take away my fear." But breath prayers do not require surgery to be useful. Anytime you are overwhelmed or feeling in over your head, breath prayers can be a way of refocusing your attention on God rather than the difficulties at hand.

Snippets of rest. Elaine has spent time recovering from a concussion twice. Concussion recovery often involves protecting the brain from mental stress as it restores its normal function. As Elaine went through this for several months, she developed a new practice of lying down

---

[20]F@W_ST59, Black man, age 49, director of operations/technology consultant, evangelical, interview conducted February 26, 2019.

[21]See F@W_ST152, Asian woman, age 27, social media manager and optometry technician, Muslim, interview conducted October 23, 2019.

[22]Denise's surgery was required to fix two congenital heart defects that she did not learn she had until middle age. God was gracious, and the defects were able to be repaired with no further damage. Her surgeon tells her that she now has a normal life expectancy!

with her eyes closed and repeating a scriptural refrain for at least five minutes three or four times a day. She was surprised by how effective this was in reorienting her toward God being in control of her life. Christian workers could try taking small breaks like this a few times during the workday rather than having just one more quick conversation or writing one more email, and in this way begin to implement a practice of rest into the workday.

Slowing the pace. Another way we can make time for rest during the workday is slowing down the pace of decision making. Often when someone presents us with a decision that needs to be made quickly, we feel an internal pressure to rush because the other person is rushing. Over time, both of us have learned to protect our time by slowing the pace with which we make decisions. At the institute Elaine directs at Rice University, for example, her work team has instituted "no-email Fridays," so team members might have some uninterrupted time to work on tasks and rest from the fervent activity of incessant email that needs to be answered. (Truth in advertising: we are only partly successful at this!) Denise is learning to assess the extent to which she actually needs to make all of the decisions that come her way. It has been surprising to learn that many things are resolved on their own without her direct intervention.

Week to week. It is important to talk about week-to-week rhythms as well. Christians may have a leg up in balancing work and rest because we have been given the scriptural example and commandment to practice Sabbath. When a weekly sabbath is practiced regularly, it reminds us of our own limitations and helps us to experience rest as a part of obedience to God and to Christian teaching.

Denise has researched how people understand and practice sabbath, and we have thought about some of the practices that infuse that day of rest. We can think of the sabbath as a day set aside in our week when we do not do our usual work or even things that remind us of our usual work. This is going to mean that we need to get set up for the sabbath in other parts of the week. It might mean slightly longer workdays during the week or letting some things go undone. Sometimes life gets in the way and, because of, for example, the need to care for others, we are not always able to take a full day. In this case, Christians might consider whether there is someone they might ask to take over their care responsibilities for an afternoon so they can fully rest for a period. While many workers might not have the flexibility to take one day off a week to reorient themselves, we find that most of us who do have the ability to take one day off from work each week do not actually take the time. It is helpful to create both intentionality and some rituals to protect that time. For example, Denise and her family currently attend church on Saturday nights and host a small group in their home on Sunday nights. Between these two events, she does not check her work email or do any work-related tasks. Elaine is not a big napper, but she finds it helpful to begin her sabbath by taking at least a thirty-minute nap after church services.

Month to month. A day a month to reorient our focus on God in our work might look like this: We would start the day with a walk to get our mind free. Then we might journal about each domain of our work. We would eat slowly. We might get together with someone at the end of the day to talk about what we have learned and how what we have learned will impact our work and rest practices moving forward.

Year to year. We also need to think about yearly rhythms. What kind of rest will be made available during the holidays? Christian workers who need to travel but find it to be energy sapping might consider how they will compensate, perhaps by making their trip shorter to allow for rest on either side. Christians who are in a leadership position in their work organization might think about the benefits of sponsoring generous vacation time for their workers.

Difference in life stages. We often hear that today's youth are lazy and do not care much for hard work—but the truth is, for as long as we have been chronicling, the older generation has critiqued the younger generation over its work habits. "The worst part is that they don't care what people—their mothers and fathers and uncles and aunts—think of them. They haven't any sense of shame, honor or duty. . . . They don't care about anything except pleasure," social scientist Sara Konrath found in an article from the 1920s about its own "modern youngsters."[23]

But some things might actually be different for young people today. Recent generations of Americans have been in school for more of their lives and have much less free time than previous generations their age.[24] Konrath, who has been following generational trends for most of her career and is known for comparing young people from different time periods to understand generational change, writes that the "younger generation isn't lazy; they are burned out."[25] She provides evidence that young people today are experiencing burnout that comes from emotional exhaustion. They are facing higher stress, are increasingly overwhelmed, and have greater symptoms of poor mental health. There are too many expectations and demands—including an always-on culture driven by social media that does not allow for rest—in addition to too few resources and too little support. There is also a decline in young people thinking that others are good and trustworthy, which is a chief symptom of burnout.[26]

Younger people are pushing for greater work-life balance, including focusing more on rest and relaxation. They have also pushed for more flexible work arrangements, such as the ability to work virtually, which can potentially create increased time for rest (time not needed to

[23]See Vivian Richardson, "What About This Flapper Generation?," *Dallas Morning News*, July 11, 1926, https://freepages.rootsweb.com/~jwheat/history/flappers.html.

[24]See Sandra L. Hofferth and John F. Sandberg, "Changers in American Children's Time, 1981–1997," *Advances in Life Course Research* 6 (2001): 193-229.

[25]Sarah Konrath, "I Study America's Youth. Here's What I Found," Big Think, September 2, 2022, https://bigthink.com/the-well/kids-youth-today/.

[26]Sara H. Konrath, "The Younger Generation Isn't Lazy; They're Burned Out," *Greater Good Magazine*, October 21, 2022, https://greatergood.berkeley.edu/article/item/the_younger_generation _isnt_lazy_theyre_burned_out.

commute or travel, for example) but run the risk of not forming meaningful relationships at work.[27] Perhaps as a result, young people may be leading the way for a "working from rest" mindset, teaching all of us how to better balance work and rest.

Caring for others' rest. Finally, many of us find ourselves in the position through our own leadership of setting rest times for others, in the form of vacation schedules and even breaks during the day. Whenever we can, we ought to lead by example in caring for our own rest and through creating structures that allow rest for others. This might mean using our power to advocate for more vacation time and other forms of flexible scheduling that start to approximate the opportunities those closer to the top of the organization receive. Theologian Walter Brueggemann writes in *The Prophetic Imagination*:

> Jesus in his solidarity with the marginal ones is moved to compassion. Compassion constitutes a radical form of criticism for it announces that the hurt is to be taken seriously, that the hurt is not to be accepted as normal and natural but is abnormal and unacceptable condition for humanness. . . . From a specifically Christian standpoint, the compassion of Jesus is not to be understood as a personal emotional reaction but as a public criticism in which he dares to act upon his concern against the entire numbness of the social context.[28]

Part of justice is actually protecting rest for others.

REFLECTION QUESTIONS

For everyone

- What is your typical pattern of work and rest? In what ways does your approach to rest align with your understanding of God's

---

[27]See Marcello Russo and Ioana Lupu, "Why Young Professionals Should Prioritize Rest over Work," *Harvard Business Review*, November 29, 2021, https://hbr.org/2021/11/why-young -professionals-should-prioritize-rest-over-work. This article discusses why, contrary to popular wisdom, people earlier in their careers should actually prioritize rest over work.

[28]Walter Brueggemann, *The Prophetic Imagination*, 40th anniversary ed. (Minneapolis: Fortress, 2018), 88.

desires for you? Are there ways you might want to approach rest differently from your current practice?

- How do you think your family's values and work practices affect your current work and rest habits?
- Do you lead others in your workplace toward more rest or less? How could you foster a workplace atmosphere that values hard and good work as well as rest from work?
- Envision an ideal system of work-life balance that incorporates the sabbath. What practices would be helpful for your organization to implement that would align it with your ideal vision?

For faith communities

- To what extent do you hear messages from your church about the value or importance of rest from work?
- What things could your church do to encourage a healthy balance between work and rest?

Epilogue

DREAMING OF THE FUTURE

"WITHOUT A DREAM about what the future *could be*, we can never be the people we *need to be* to walk toward that future," Elaine's pastor once told her. Ultimately, that is how we want to end this book: by imagining a new future of faith in the workplace. We want to see our scholarship and Christian thinking used to bring true changes to how Christians live out their faith at work. To this end, we outline our hopes for different audiences of this book: church and parachurch leaders, workplace leaders, and everyone who works.

OUR MESSAGE FOR CHURCH LEADERS

In their ideal form, churches are special organizations in society where people from different places in life and different occupations come together. Church ought to be a place for safe conversations and mentoring on how to thrive and be used by God at work, free from the hierarchies and constraints that are present on the job. We want to see pastors and church leaders clearly communicate how nearly all work can be experienced as a calling. Expand discussions about calling to include the self, others, and the workplace more generally—and how all workers have the power to use their work in service to God and others. Second, we want to see church leaders have a broad vision of how they can better help and support workers, even those who do work that is not viewed as prestigious by society, while also cultivating among those who are at the top of their organizations a spirit of discipleship and discernment. In particular, listen to your congregants to understand whether they have been marginalized at work because of their faith, even if such treatment does not rise to the legal threshold of discrimination.

The pastor's voice may be more powerful than pastors realize. Use sermons to illustrate ways that workers have affected positive change in their organizations and explore the ways that congregants might be able to implement changes that would better align their workplaces with kingdom values.

OUR MESSAGE FOR WORKPLACE LEADERS

Leaders must allow time for rest, reflection, and relationships in and outside work, both for themselves and for others. Since the start of the pandemic, we recognize even more than before that not all of life is about work and that people desire both to work and to have time to fully experience other aspects of their lives. We want to see Christian organizational leaders expand their imagination for what it means to lead an organization where Christian faith acts as leavening: the best yeast does not sit off to the side; bread is leavened or made capable of rising only when the yeast is fully worked into the dough. We think the healthiest perspective for an organization is one where Christians are leavening rather than separatist. We want Christian leaders to think about every aspect of their organization and all of the people in it, not just the pieces they think are "specifically Christian" or for only the Christians in the organization. Part of allowing people to bring their entire selves to work requires fostering an environment where it is safe to have appropriate conversations about religion in a way that supports, not undermines, organizational goals. This includes understanding how religious discrimination operates in your field, occupation, and particular workplace.

Christian leaders also need to create a space for all those in their organization to realize their gifts. We want to see Christian leaders be supportive of the work that each person does, encourage everyone in the organization to think about their gifts in the context of their calling, and talk with others in the workplace about what they value and what challenges the workplace creates.

Organizational leaders can also help their workers by creating a workplace culture that supports healthy patterns of work and rest. This can include policies that help workers set boundaries on their work time to avoid burnout or allow opportunities for restoration, such as breaks for walks, exercise, or even prayer. In short, those who are in power need to ensure that those throughout the system—from the lowest to the highest positions—have opportunities for rest. It is not just we who are protecting ourselves by punctuating our work with rest; we are also protecting others and recognizing their need to rest as well.

In our vision of the future, Christian workers will fully recognize their own humanity and the humanity of others. Deep appreciation for the other, we have found, will come when we appreciate the humanness of the other, when we do not turn away from suffering but recognize in the other an individual who is also made in the image of God.

OUR MESSAGE FOR EVERY WORKER

Start by telling yourself, "I am fully loved by God." Repeat that as many times a day as you need to. In one sense, because you are fully loved, you do not need to prove anything. Christian workers should also take time to reflect on their gifts and propensities. Ask yourself, "What is the best version of myself?" Take time to know how God has created you to experience pleasure in particular kinds of work. What are the things you are doing that give you the greatest sense of feeling God's pleasure? We know that, given all the difficulties workers face and the constraints placed on work, it is not always possible to pursue your ideal work. But our hope for Christian workers is that they will take the time and energy to understand their true giftings and propensities and to hone these giftings. Start with focusing on the things you love. We also hope that Christian workers can come to use these gifts in their church community.

We want to see Christian workers value and dignify all people by helping to protect those from other faiths at work and ensuring that value, dignity, and religious expression are equally recognized and respected for everyone in the workplace. Our faith fundamentally demands nothing less. Speak out against comments or behaviors that are critical of someone's religious practices or beliefs, whether these comments are directed at you or at someone else, and take action against discrimination, whether directed at you or at others.

May God bless you as you carry what you have learned from this book into your workplace. May you recognize your own gifts and callings at work in service to God and others. May you see God's image in every person at work and seek to communicate their value and dignity. May you recognize and use the power you have to make changes in situations and systems that are counter to God's kingdom. May you encourage the development of God-given gifts for every person with whom you work. May you stand firm and humble in the faith, and live out your faith at work in such a way that God is honored. May you experience the gift of resting from your work. And may God bless you as you seek to be a blessing to others.

Appendix

THE RESEARCH
BEHIND THIS BOOK

METHODOLOGY

Working for Better is based on data from two connected studies that were funded by the Lilly Endowment: (1) the Faith at Work Study, which provided our primary dataset; and (2) the Faith at Work Supplement Study, which was conducted during Covid-19 to give us additional insight into the impacts of the pandemic on faith at work. We have a book targeted to a secular academic audience, *Religion in a Changing Workplace* (Oxford University Press, 2024), where we have published the entire surveys and interview guide. We do different analyses for the two books, but for readers who are interested in even more detail about the methods of the two studies, particularly the two surveys we used, we encourage a look at that book as well.

FAITH AT WORK STUDY

The Faith at Work Study included three phases: (1) focus groups: we conducted six focus groups with Christian workers and three with pastors in Houston, New York, and Seattle; (2) survey: we conducted a broad-based general US population survey; and (3) interviews: we followed up our survey with in-depth interviews, examining how people understand and integrate faith and work.

Survey. The survey was fielded from October 2, 2018, to December 15, 2018, using the Gallup Panel, a probability-based panel of US adults who are recruited using random digit-dial (RDD) phone interviews that cover landlines and cellphones and address-based sampling methods (ABS). A stratified sample of 29,345 US adults was drawn from the Gallup Panel. The demographic distribution of the sample matched the US population targets for US adults obtained from the 2017 Current Population Survey. Additionally, the stratified sample included oversamples of 752 pre-identified Muslim and 882 pre-identified Jewish respondents. By mode, 24,534 web- and 4,811 mail-panel members were sampled. By language, 27,766 English- and 1,579 Spanish-panel members were sampled.

A total of 13,270 people completed the survey. This equates to an overall completion rate of 45.2 percent. This completion rate was higher among the Jewish subsample (65 percent) and lower among the Muslim subsample (27 percent).

Interviews. Interviews occurred during project years two and three. In total, we interviewed 182 workers from our survey who—based on their survey responses—stated that they were working full time, part time, or not currently working but looking for work; who identified with a religious tradition; and who were at least somewhat active in a religious community based on their frequency of religious service attendance. We also interviewed twelve nonreligious workers from our survey. We selected all interview subjects with the goal of ensuring a representative distribution across gender, race, and ethnicity. In the end, we analyzed 194 interviews of survey respondents, which included a majority of Christian workers, in addition to smaller numbers of Muslim and Jewish workers and those with no religion.

We also interviewed forty-two pastors. Most were identified through clergy databases provided by Made to Flourish, as well as the Religion in Public Life Center at Rice University.

FAITH AT WORK SUPPLEMENT STUDY

The Faith at Work Supplement Study was designed to assess how two emergent crises—the Covid-19 pandemic and racial conflict in the United States—were shaping the relationship between faith and work for US adults. This supplemental project included a population survey and in-depth interviews to explore the nuanced implications—including the social, economic, and spiritual realities—of these crises in the lives of workers and the faith leaders who work and serve among them.

Survey. The survey for the Faith at Work Supplement Study was fielded from September 7, 2021, to October 4, 2021. US adults were selected from the Gallup Panel, a probability-based panel of US adults that is recruited using random digit-dial (RDD) phone interviews that cover landlines and cellphones and address-based sampling methods (ABS). Gallup statisticians in total drew a sample of 9,299 adults, age eighteen and older. A total of 2,486 people completed the survey. This equates to an overall completion rate of 26.7 percent. Response rates for panel surveys must take into account all stages of selection into the sample, which occurs in stages.

Interviews. At the end of the survey, respondents were asked whether they would be willing to be recontacted for a follow-up interview, and 1,405 agreed. Gallup provided the contact information for these survey takers. We contacted 107 survey takers to participate in follow-up interviews with the goal of generating a racially and religiously diverse sample of interview subjects. Fifty-one survey respondents completed interviews. Between the two studies and including interviews with pastors, we conducted a total of 287 interviews.

Table A.1 shows some of the demographic characteristics of the people who responded to our surveys.

Table A.1. Demographic information of respondents

Sample descriptors—demographic variables

VARIABLE	CATEGORY	PERCENTAGE OF FULL SAMPLE
Religion	Evangelical	16
	Mainline Protestant	16
	Catholic	17
	Other Christian	15
	Jewish	2
	Muslim	1
	None	28
	Other	5
Gender	Male	48
	Female	51
Organizational Position	Top	17
	Middle	47
	Bottom	36
	Business & Legal	18
Occupational Category	Arts, Culture, and Humanities	15
	STEM and Technical Jobs	15
	Health and Social Services	13
	Other	39

Data is from the Faith at Work main and supplementary surveys. This table displays percentages of the total sample by demographics. The total sample has $N = 15{,}756$ individuals.

INDEX